THE DOLLHOUSE BOOK

Plate 1.   Clare's Early American Dollhouse is decorated in warm colors with simple fabrics to give it a homespun look. The downstairs rooms have exposed beams, and the furniture is straight and functional. Where decorations are used they are a Pennsylvania Dutch style.

Plate 2.   Anne's French Provincial Dollhouse is decorated and furnished in the elaborate but elegant Georgian style. The curved furniture is painted white and decorated with gold. Satin fabrics and gold braids help to give the house a look of wealth and taste associated with the 18th century.

Plate 3.   Elizabeth's Victorian Dollhouse is decorated in the extravagant manner of the 19th century. The windows are heavily draped, and the rooms are filled with overstuffed furniture, potted plants, and bric-a-brac. The walls are covered with figured fabrics, and the ceilings are decorated with delicate gold decals.

Plate 4.   The Portable Box Room is elaborately decorated in the manner of a theatrical dressing room. The brocade draperies are heavily trimmed with tassels and braid. The walls are velvet and the furniture is curved and gilded. The doors are designed to hold the "star's" costumes.

The

Dollhouse

Book

ESTELLE ANSLEY WORRELL

Basic House Plans and Photography by
NORMAN WORRELL

VNR VAN NOSTRAND REINHOLD COMPANY
NEW YORK CINCINNATI TORONTO LONDON MELBOURNE

Van Nostrand Reinhold Company Regional Offices:
New York, Cincinnati, Chicago, Millbrae, Dallas

Van Nostrand Reinhold Company International Offices:
London, Toronto, Melbourne

Copyright © 1964 by ESTELLE ANSLEY WORRELL
Library of Congress Catalog Card Number 64-57228
ISBN 0-442-29558-8 — paper edition
ISBN 0-442-09550-3 — cloth edition

Published by Van Nostrand Reinhold Company
A Division of Litton Educational Publishing, Inc.
450 West 33rd Street, New York, N.Y. 10001

Published simultaneously in Canada by
Van Nostrand Reinhold Limited

13   15   16   14   12

Preface

In early fall three years ago my husband, Norman Worrell, and I decided to give our two daughters a dollhouse for Christmas. After shopping a while, it became evident that a large permanent dollhouse was not to be easily found. The only solution seemed to be to have one made. Norman, a professional designer, insisted that design research must be the first step.

The more we read on dollhouse history the more excited we became! Before long we had planned that each daughter must have her own personal dollhouse.

We worked out a scale, Norman designed the basic cabinet, and I began to make plans for the furnishings. By Christmas that same year, we had two dollhouses complete enough to put beside the Christmas tree—and another daughter, two weeks old!

By spring, I had made so many penciled patterns of doll furniture for friends that I knew I must write an article about our project. We started another house for our youngest (we knew I could use it until she became old enough for it) and went to see Jay Hedden, editor of *Workbench* magazine. He not only bought the story but helped me in so many ways that this book might never have been published without him.

Before I knew it, there were newspaper stories and TV shows, and people were calling me the "lady who makes the dollhouses." Bette Hayes of WDAF-TV invited me to appear on her show a total of seven times during the next year, and she and her many viewers gave me an insight into their wants and needs that I couldn't have found any other way. One of those viewers, Valeda Huber, designed the "steamer trunk" style dollhouse and knew where to locate more miniatures than I knew existed.

In the meantime, my friends and neighbors not only forgave me for my neglect but saved odds and ends and brought gifts to us which they "just happened to run across."

My daughters helped me in a million ways—doing everything from listening for the baby Clare to actually helping with the miniatures. Most of all, they helped by spending hours with their friends playing with the dollhouses.

The book gradually took form and became such a family affair that even the grandparents began making miniatures. Once as I watched my mother whip lace onto tiny bed pillows and sheets while my daughters and I worked on rugs, it occurred to me that here is a project that knows no age limits. With father and grandfather interpreting the patterns with power tools, brother using them with hand tools as a Scout project, and the girls of all ages fascinated with making a dollhouse fit for a princess, this could be a lifetime hobby for the whole family!

This book grew out of a genuine desire to share my discoveries and ideas with other families and particularly with people who have limited tools and work space but who enjoy creating things. Had I made the remark three years ago that I wanted to design an "elaborate dollhouse which could be made simply and inexpensively," my friends would not have believed me. Now they share their own "elaborate yet simple" ideas with me.

I hope that this book will enable people of all ages to create and enjoy a beautiful and individual dollhouse.

ESTELLE ANSLEY WORRELL

Contents

[*vii*]

List of Illustrations

1

Dollhouses of the Past

The toys we have during our childhood always influence our lives because there are so many memories associated with them. Sometimes the toys that stand out in our memories are simple and inexpensive, but most often they are the fine quality ones that were able to withstand years of play. Of all toys, probably none has as fabulous a history as the dollhouse. Some historians insist that they date back to Egyptian days but all agree that they go back at least to the early seventeenth century.

The museum examples of this early type are made in the cabinet style. It is believed that these first dollhouses originated in Germany. They often had four rooms, two on a lower floor and two on an upper floor. These rooms were protected by large doors which opened on the front. Some examples have had four doors, one for each room! There was usually a pediment, or some type of roof to give it an architectural feeling. The wood was left natural inside the rooms as well as on the cabinet exterior. The doors were hung by large leather strap hinges. The estate carpenter usually constructed these cabinets, and sometimes his sense of scale, or lack of it, gave them a special charm. Sometimes his doors, windows, and mantels were very large in proportion to the furnishings to be used in the dollhouse, and this gave them a childlike appearance.

Probably only the very wealthy families had dollhouses made for their children in those early days. Early dollhouses might have been built mainly for housing miniature sets of pots and pans, furniture, and dishes. Note the elaborate sets of kitchen equipment in the one-room dollhouse in plate No. 5. These sets were made by furniture makers and smiths who made miniature samples of their wares to show to prospective buyers. They rode from village to village on horseback, and it was impossible to carry their actual products because of their size. These sample sets eventually were sold for toys, and the dollhouse evolved as a result.

The dollhouse was originally called a "baby house" because a doll was called a "child's toy baby." Many dictionaries still define "doll" the same way. Because of

Plate 5. An early "Nuremberg Kitchen" is elaborately furnished with all the domestic equipment needed to run a kitchen. Note the matched sets of mugs, plates, etc. and the long handled utensils and tools on the back wall. Victoria and Albert Museum, Crown Copyright.

Plate 6.   The Blackett Baby House is dated at about 1740. The festooned curtains and the painted wallpapers are original. The basement rooms are reached through doors on the sides. The staircase is within the fixed central panel. The London Museum, London.

[*3*]

the very character of dollhouses, they have survived the centuries better than most other types of toys.

The early miniatures made in the American colonies were made by craftsmen from tin scraps left over from real utensils. These were scarce because only necessary things were bought or made until the end of the century.

During the eighteenth century in Europe, it was not uncommon for a wealthy father to build the dollhouse himself during the long winter months when the family was isolated in the castle. This seems to have been particularly true in England. By this time, the colonists in America were beginning to import English toys because of their new wealth and leisure.

Eighteenth century dollhouses began to have stairs added, as well as elaborate mantels, and exterior architectural features as shown in plate No. 6. Builders began to paint them both inside and out. When wallpapers became popular, they were used in the dollhouses too. The basic cabinet style was retained, yet they began to look more like houses. There are stories about some antique houses of this period which are believed to be actual copies of the owners' real homes.

Locks were usually installed in the doors in order to protect the valuable silver, pewter, and china miniature collections. Some dollhouses had a front panel which could be removed instead of doors. These panels usually had locks also. These locks have led historians to believe that the houses were only unlocked for the children on special occasions.

This eighteenth century cabinet with realistic doors, windows, pediments, and other architectural features was the perfect combination of beauty and function. By possessing the best features of the cabinet style and the architectural style, these houses came very near to meeting all the needs of both child and adult owners who would be concerned with them.

Many of the dolls of this period were actually made for milliners and dressmakers to be used for samples of their work. Miniature implements were made of pewter. They were still being made by the makers of the real articles as a sideline for samples, premiums, and advertisement.

By the time the nineteenth century had come along, dollhouses had become more architectural in shape. Toward the end of the century, many were charming miniatures of actual houses. They were elaborately constructed with a variety of carpenter's materials. There were a few dollhouses manufactured during this period but none were sold on a large scale. The London Exhibition of 1851 had a great number of dollhouses and miniatures. Some had storage drawers and stands to go with them. Most of them were of permanent wood construction and good quality. It has been stated that the great popularity of the miniatures sold at the Exhibition could be partly

Plate 7.   The Lansdowne Doll's House of 1860 has a red brick facade, and the pediment has the Royal Arms of Queen Victoria. The stairway and the front panels can be removed to reveal the basement rooms. The basement rooms are the kitchen and the nursery. The London Museum, London.

attributed to the fact that so many adults bought them for themselves for bric-a-brac. There are still many fine china, brass, and copper miniatures made in England today. Almost any American gift shop has at least a few on the shelves.

The nineteenth century had brought wealth to many Americans so they could buy such luxuries as fine toys, and many of their beautiful old dollhouses are found in our museums now. The architectural style was well suited to the spacious Victorian

[5]

Plate 8. The Lansdowne Doll's House interiors are beautifully furnished. The stairway climbs up three floors through a center hallway. Note the doors with their curtained windows. The London Museum, London.

[6]

mansions in which they were kept. There were still many cabinet-style dollhouses being made during the nineteenth century, however, as evidenced by plates No. 7 and 8. This dollhouse, probably more than any other, influenced my decision to design cabinets for my own three daughters.

In America about this time, lovely Victorian cabinets were being made such as the Annie C. Warren dollhouse, plate No. 10, and the one made for Bessie Lincoln a little later, plate No. 11. Note the interesting attics and gables.

In England in 1879 a young twelve-year-old, Princess May of Teck, received a lovely cabinet dollhouse which may very well have been the beginning of her life-long love for dollhouses. See plate No. 9. In her adult life, as Queen Mary, she commissioned the fabulous Queen Mary's Dolls' House known all over the world.

The twentieth century does have manufactured dollhouses but few of permanent quality. Many are small-scale houses of tin or cardboard with painted architectural features. The few wooden houses manufactured are mostly made on a small scale and are expensive. There are a few, however, that are beginning to be made large enough for the popular dolls, and these are well designed. Manufacturers seem to have forgotten the lovely space-saving cabinet style.

Fabulous dollhouses of the past were made or commissioned for a particular person by a carpenter or loving relative or friend. These fortunate owners were usually wealthy so the dollhouses were expensively and beautifully made. Even today any really outstanding dollhouse is made in much the same manner. A dollhouse is a very personal possession and should reflect the taste and needs of its owner just as a home should. For this reason they are valuable historically. They usually copy contemporary life. The contemporary dollhouses shown in the following chapters reflect our present fascination with our own American past, and at the same time make use of today's materials and methods of construction.

Plate 9.   Princess May of Teck's Doll's House still has the furniture acquired by the Princess (who later became Queen Mary). It was made in 1879 when the Princess was 12 years old. Note the bay windows built into the doors. The London Museum, London.

[8]

Plate 10.   The Warren Dollhouse was made for the children of Annie Crownin-shield Warren in 1852. The rug in the drawing room (right, center) was worked by Mrs. Warren to represent an Aubusson rug, and she also embroidered the fire screen. Note the interesting roof. Essex Institute, Salem, Mass.

Plate 11.   The Bessie Lincoln Dollhouse was built in Salem, Mass., in 1876.
The attic and the base with drawers provide plenty of storage space. Note the homey
American quality of the ruffled curtains, checkered draperies, and the well equipped
kitchen. Essex Institute, Salem, Mass.

2

Dollhouses of Today

We have a way of accepting tradition without questioning it. The so-called "traditional 1″ to 1′ scale" is still used by many dollhouse manufacturers, although it probably started out of convenience for furniture makers and smiths who made miniature samples to show prospective buyers. What scale is simpler and requires less mathematics than one inch on the sample for every one foot on the full size article?

Today toy manufacturers produce millions of 7″ to 12″ dolls without a permanent house of that scale. They don't make houses for dolls, the dolls must be made for the houses. A doll small enough to fit a 1″ scale house is so small that its clothes are usually glued or sewn right onto it. Their bodies are seldom jointed or realistic. On the other hand, the popular 7″ to 12″ dolls have a huge amount of miniatures and clothes made especially for them and not a permanent home in which to live! There are also a great many antique dolls which are in this same scale.

Another interesting contradiction is the fact that when only wealthy persons who lived in grand homes had dollhouses, they were a cabinet type which took up little space. Today when dwellers in small suburban homes can afford fine dollhouses, the few available ones are the kind that have to sit in the middle of the room or that open from the back and require a large table.

The author's basic dollhouse cabinet was designed with three main factors in mind. First, of course, was the size of the dolls most cherished by young girls. These beloved dolls which young girls collect in great numbers fall into a 7″ to 12″ scale.

Designers use what is known as a human engineering chart for reference. It is a compilation of statistics which supplies information such as the length of the average woman's hands (this is important if you are designing a kitchen gadget), or how long an average man's legs are (for designing an easy chair, etc.). A kind of doll engineering scale was worked out for this large group of dolls from 7″ to 12″. This scale was used for the furnishings in the same manner, using both the dolls and the house. It was not possible to arrive at an exact mathematical scale because the dolls vary slightly in proportion, especially their heads. The scale was arrived at "by eye," so to speak. Most of the proportions used fall into a 2″ to 1′ scale most of the time, however.

The second factor to be considered, after the size of the future occupant, was the size of the future owner. Comfort and ease were most important. The owner should be able to reach all the rooms without bending and stretching. A base was designed to raise the house up so that the lower floor would be high enough to be easy to reach into, but not so high that the upper floor would be awkward to reach. This base also provides knee and toe room because it is recessed. For variations of the base, such as a drawer, legs, etc., see variations sketches.

The top was left flat with a pediment attached for looks. This suggestion of a pediment is a reminder that although it is an attractive cabinet, it is still a dollhouse. It was decided that the top could be used for setting things on. This has proved to be a very special feature because it helps to keep the miniatures off the floor. Some furnishings are always removed during use, and they don't get stepped on, lost, or sucked into the vacuum if they are put on top.

An attic room can be built on top for storage or for another room. It was not used on the basic house plan, however, because of the fact that it is difficult to reach all three floors from one position.

The home in which the dollhouse was to be placed was the third consideration. A four-foot-square dollhouse can be a real problem in a small room. A depth of 15″ was decided on so that the cabinet could be treated as a bookcase or chest. It stands back against the wall and takes up little floor space. The rooms are high and wide, but relatively shallow in proportion; this allows every part of them to be easily reached. Some early European dollhouses have banister railings along the open side of the rooms to prevent things from being knocked out. Ironically, these banisters are almost always themselves damaged!

The doors have very important functional uses as anyone who has a cat will know. Puppies, too, can be a menace to dollhouses if they are left within reach. Since many pre-school children can be destructive also, a lock can be installed in the doors as was done in the seventeenth and eighteenth centuries. A lock and key will give the owner a special sense of ownership and pride as well as protect the house and furnishings from harm. Since dust is as much a problem in dollhouses as in our homes, the doors serve a real purpose. If the doors are kept closed when the dollhouse is not being used, it can go for months without dusting.

Probably the feature with the greatest appeal to adults is the exterior treatment. By looking more like a piece of furniture than a house, it can blend perfectly with the furniture in the room where it is to be kept. In the case of adult collectors, this can well be a living or dining room. There are many types of doors and finishes which can

Plate 12.   The basic cabinet shown here is a combination of all the features which have proven to be the most functional during the author's three years of living with the dollhouses and using them. The other cabinets will vary slightly because they were experimental.

be used on the cabinet such as louvered doors, the open frame door, which can be filled with a fabric to match the room's color scheme, and even glass doors. Various legs, bases, and drawers can be used, and there is a variety of hardware to be purchased. When the room, the dollhouse cabinet, and its furnishings all are the same style, the result is pleasing and harmonious.

This exterior treatment also simplifies the storage problem during years when the dollhouse may not be used. The doors will help to protect it from dust, insects, unappreciative children, pets, and so on. As a display case or piece of furniture, the dollhouse can still have a prized miniature added to it from time to time, and it can be viewed but not disturbed.

When legs are used, the 4″ x 40½″ base strip should not be recessed, but should be moved to the front so that the legs can be installed behind it.

When covering the interior walls of all types of dollhouses, it will be much easier

[*13*]

to use fabric than paper. It is less expensive than paper also. Inexpensive cotton percale, denim, and corduroy work best. When using 36″ wide fabric, use one yard for each room. Make the joint in a corner so it won't show. Paint the walls with white glue and apply cloth carefully. There will be about a quarter of a yard left over which can be used for bedcovers, upholstery, or doll clothes.

Use ribbon, braid, or lace for the ceiling border and also for the floor molding if one is needed. See interior photographs in plates 1, 2, 3, and 4 for individual wall treatments and furnishings. Small wood moldings can be used around the floor and ceiling for an architectural treatment. This can be done when the house is constructed or later, and is quite elegant and realistic.

The owner's name and the date can be put right on the house by carving, woodburning, or by attaching a metal nameplate. This can be done on the pediment, doors, over a mantel, or on the top or bottom of the cabinet. It will be treasured by future generations when the house is handed down.

INDIVIDUAL BOX ROOMS

Individual box rooms, the same scale as the rooms in the basic cabinet, can be made. They are easier to construct than the cabinet because only a hammer, nails, and glue are needed. The plywood can be cut to size by the lumber company, and the rooms can be assembled by a person with little or no experience in woodworking.

Besides being simple to construct, they are portable. They can be made a room at a time and can even be gift wrapped! A house can be completed over a period of months or years, and any number of rooms can be stacked together in numerous arrangements. They can even be used as additions to the basic house. When several persons in a family must share the house, this type can give a sense of ownership by allowing each individual his or her own box room within the total arrangement.

When the owner is confined to bed during illness, this box room can be enjoyed right on the bed. When a handle is put on top, it can be transported.

Doors can be added to each box. Be sure that both right and left doors are used so that when stacked, they won't be in the way. Double doors can be used also. See variations sketches.

The handle on top of each room should be the type of drawer pull which lies flat when not in use. (This type of handle can be bought in any style at most hardware counters.) Use four rubber tips on the bottom of each room to hold it above the handle of the one below. This will prevent slipping when stacked. Besides giving a finished look to the box, these tips will also prevent its scratching any furniture on which it is placed.

When the handle is put on, be sure to place it about ½″ closer to the front than

Plate 13.   The individual box room is shown here with double doors. It has a small latch for keeping the furnishings securely inside during moving. It has rubber bumper tips on the bottom to prevent slipping or scratching furniture.

the back. This will make the box tilt just slightly to the back when picked up so that anything that falls will fall into the room instead of out of the opening. This is important whether doors are added or not.

Many small boys like minatures as well as girls. This single box room can be used for a garage, store, stable, school, boathouse, and many other things. A number of toy cars are on the market which are perfectly proportioned to the dollhouse. Miniature tool kits and gas station equipment kits can be found in dime stores. A box room project of his own will keep a boy from feeling left out of the family game of miniature collecting and save wear and tear on the dollhouse.

The walls of the box room shown in plate No. 4 are covered with pink velvet. The ceiling border is a heavy beige lace. The chandelier is made of iridescent beads. The curtains are gold brocade and chiffon.

The vanity and the Louis XV chair patterns are in the French Provincial pattern section. The folding screen and accessories are described on the accessory pages.

[*15*]

Plate 14.   The individual box room is made of corrugated cardboard here. It is sitting on a small end table. A small wood block holds the screws for the handle and the chandelier. The box is covered both on the inside and out with corduroy.

CORRUGATED CARDBOARD ROOM

The box can be made in corrugated cardboard also. This type is simple and inexpensive and requires only scissors and a razor blade. Two large boxes are needed for the cardboard. Cereal, detergent, or tissue boxes which can be found at the grocery store are suitable.

When constructed as directed, this dollhouse room will be surprisingly sturdy and can be kept for many years just as the wooden ones can be. It does have one definite advantage over the wooden ones: it is much lighter! A handle can be put on top if a small piece of wood or metal is used on the inside to prevent the screws from pulling through. An old plastic or leather belt can be used for a strap too. Cut small tight openings for the straps, cut the belt in half, and put ends through the holes. Roll the cut ends and sew, or fasten in some other manner so that they will not slip through.

There are many boxes very near the size of the room desired, and these can be decorated if you do not wish to construct a box. Cover both the inside and out with fabric as described in the directions for making the cardboard box room.

3

Dollhouse Furniture

The dollhouse furniture presented in the following chapters does not so much represent the *doll* furniture of the three centuries but the actual full size furniture of those periods. All the interiors and furnishings are based on research of antiques, not miniatures.

Although most of the furniture designs can easily be adapted to wood and power tools, they are intended for simple materials and household tools such as kitchen knives, scissors, and razor blades. A pair of cutting pliers will help a great deal, but they are not absolutely essential. Sandpaper, paint, and shellac are needed for many of the pieces of furniture.

The basic materials used are white glue, fabric, styrofoam, balsa wood, cardboard, clothespins, sequin pins, and match stems. It is suggested that you buy the glue in a pint jar and use a small brush for best results. Just wash the brush in cold water after use. Be sure to use white glue because it can be used for all the materials mentioned. All glues cannot be used with as many different materials and therefore are not recommended here. There are several brands. Just ask for "liquid white glue." The short ½" pin is recommended instead of the longer straight pin which bends too easily.

Many odds and ends from around the house are used, but it should be noted that discards are never used just for the sake of using them. They are used only when they can fill a need better than another material. The cartons and boxes are used because a whole step is eliminated in the construction of the furniture piece. This not only makes it easier but saves time.

The plans are made for the three houses so that if a material is not available for an item for one living room, for instance, one of the other two styles may call for the very thing you happen to have. This plan enables you to furnish an entire house for a few dollars or, if preferred, for many times that amount!

Everything shown in the houses came from the dime store, the drug store, or the grocery store. (There are a few miniatures shown in the pictures which came from gift stores or souvenir shops in order to point out these sources, but the same item is always shown elsewhere in a homemade version.) Lumber yards and art stores have many other things which can enhance the dollhouse, but they are not necessary.

All the furnishings can be mixed or matched with the commercially made furniture sold in most toy stores, and they are not only authentic but permanent also.

There are pieces of homemade furniture in some antique dollhouses. You can imagine my delight at discovering that a hundred years ago someone fashioned doll furniture from pasteboard and silk! Little has changed except the quality of the glue and cardboard.

The use of styrofoam for seats and the undersides of tables allows one, without tools, to attach legs to the furniture. Since attaching pedestals or legs has always been the biggest problem in constructing homemade doll furniture, this has proved to be of great assistance. The styrofoam is also used in cabinets, beds, and mantels to facilitate construction. It is always covered with another material, and this combination gives a permanent hardness that can be surprising. The use of muslin for the first upholstery gives the styrofoam and cardboard the firmness of wood.

For the first attempt at upholstering it will be best to use a printed fabric since little inaccuracies are unnoticed because of the design. For best results, paint or cover the surface completely with white glue before applying surface material as directed.

The use of laminated cardboard for the furniture offers limitless possibilities. As you know, plywood is made with several thin layers of wood glued and pressed together in alternating directions. Laminated furniture is made with layers of wood steamed, glued, and pressed together in the shape desired. Once it dries in that shape, it remains that way. The cardboard doll furniture made in this fashion can be made more realistic than wood furniture because it can be shaped much more than the patterns indicate. It was necessary to keep the patterns simple and easy to follow. A person who likes to experiment can make curved backs, legs, seats, and so on for more authenticity. This sculpturing (bending) should be done while gluing and then pressed in some manner till dry. When designing your own, look at real furniture for ideas of where to bend.

Each furniture pattern gives a preference for a certain material in the instructions, but this is done in order to keep things organized and easy to follow. In fact, most of the patterns can be made in any of several materials by any of a number of methods. Many of the pattern pieces are interchangeable with those on another pattern with slight alterations. The possibilities are numerous. Coffee tables and benches can be made by using the front leg patterns of some of the chairs. Bed headboards can be made by using some of the chair backs as patterns. Square tables can be lengthened, long ones can be shortened. The couches can be shortened so that they become love seats, chairs can be lengthened to become couches. Other uses can be found for many of the pattern pieces with a little imagination. It is a good idea to scan all the patterns before starting to work in order to stimulate your imagination and to find which are best suited to your taste and ability.

It is recommended that in the beginning you follow the directions carefully. After several pieces have been tried, experiment by combining patterns and materials and design your own. Discover new materials for yourself and new uses for the old ones. Remember that whenever you are in doubt about size or proportion, get a doll and perhaps another piece of furniture, place them beside the pattern or whatever you are working with, and rely on your eyes and your good judgment. If it looks right, then it is. Your sense of proportion and design is probably far better than you think. Remember that making a dollhouse should be a happy experience for all concerned.

When using a variety of materials, a gloss enamel should be used for painting. Browns which imitate wood tones can be purchased in any dime store. Gloss enamel is recommended because flat paint gets dirty with handling and is not as permanent nor as elegant looking. Keep your small brush in a jar of water when not in use. It isn't necessary to clean it each time. This hint is probably the time and trouble saver you will enjoy the most. Just remove the brush from the water, blot it, paint with it, then put it back into the water! It is always ready to use and can be put away on a moment's notice. Use a cheap little water-color brush because the metal will eventually rust, and the brush can be thrown away when the dollhouse is finished. These brushes cost only a few cents apiece, and one can be kept for each color you plan to use. Clip the brush to the side of your jar with a clip clothes pin so that the bristles are suspended in the water, not bent on the bottom of the jar.

Balsa wood, plywood, and laminated cardboard are interchangeable. When using one other than that specified by the pattern, be sure to make the proper allowances for the thickness of the material. Balsa wood was used a great deal in the Early American house in order to give a natural wood finish different from that of the dark brown enameled pieces in the Victorian one. Actually, all those balsa wood pieces can be made with laminated cardboard if brown paint is used, and they will be just as attractive. One basic finish was used in each of the three houses for contrast, but when only one house is made, several finishes can be used together as in a real home.

All the furniture made from cartons and boxes can be made from plain cardboard. Use a piece of ½″ thick styrofoam or several layers of cardboard for the bottom (this should correspond to the bottom of a box). This will give you something to pin and glue the cardboard to. Score the lines to be bent with a scissors point so that they will bend neatly. From that point on, the method will be the same as that given on the pattern.

[20]

In order to prevent damage to the book while using the patterns, it is a good idea to buy a package of light colored tissue paper for a few cents and use it for tracing the patterns. Remember to trace carefully. When cutting the patterns it will help to fold them in half first. This makes the cutting go faster and keeps your pattern accurate. Be sure to label your patterns with a pencil and store them in an envelope for future use. Then you won't have to make them again. Glue a large envelope into the back of the book like a library card envelope for this purpose.

Dollhouses and doll furniture have always imitated full-scale homes and furniture. Americans today are enthusiastically copying the designs connected with our history. While reflecting the past, the designs in the following chapters at the same time reflect today's interests. I had so much fun doing the research for the designs that the desire to share this background with readers in the following chapters was a natural outgrowth. We always appreciate something more when we understand why it is made the way it is. Even people who pretend to care little for history are intrigued by household objects connected with daily living because they give insight into what it must have been like to live in certain periods of the past.

4

A Seventeenth Century
Early American Dollhouse

SEVENTEENTH CENTURY DESIGN BACKGROUND

During the first hard years in Virginia and Masachusetts the settlers lived in temporary crude huts with dirt floors. As they acquired tools and more time in which to use them, they began to build permanent houses for comfort and beauty.

Soon William Bradford and Myles Standish were becoming well known. Boston, Salem, and Jamestown were growing fast. Sawmills had been started, and brick makers and tinsmiths were busy making necessary building materials and household implements.

Houses were copied from those built in England during Queen Elizabeth's reign, but the unlimited supply of lumber and the fact that they were built from memory helped these cottages take on a new look that was strictly American.

Since the early builders were not always sure just how large to make the supporting beams, they naturally made them much larger than necessary. For this reason they have gained strength through the years until they are like steel today. These great beams were always left exposed and in a natural finish. The inside walls were vertical planks while the outside walls were horizontal boards known as clapboard.

The earliest furniture was copied from that in England, Holland, and Germany. Stools, trestle and sawbuck tables, benches, four-poster beds, cradles, and heavy chests were used. This furniture had straight lines with carving and wood-turned decorations. There was little softness except a few cushions, and most pieces were not especially comfortable. Upholstered furniture was not introduced until the latter part of the seventeenth century. The first upholstered pieces were covered in leather or "turkey work," a crude homemade needlework.

There was no living room furniture as we know it today because the early living rooms were the kitchens as well as the dining rooms. The huge stone fireplaces for warmth and for cooking dominated these rooms. Seats for more than one person

[*22*]

were at first just extended stools, or benches. Later, backs were added, then arms, so that they became settees. Crewelwork upholstery was later added to the William and Mary settees, and the couch or sofa eventually came into popularity near the end of the century.

Accessories of the period were those things which were necessary to life such as spinning wheels, wrought-iron and brass fireplace accessories, pewter cups and plates, lanterns, candlesticks, copper kitchen wares, and warming pans. Guns were usually hung on the walls and a few pictures and maps. Oriental rugs were imported but were used as table covers and wall hangings instead of on the floor. The earliest rugs made in the Colonies were rag and braided ones. Some were also knitted and crocheted in circles and ovals.

Crewelwork, knitted items, and crochet work were popular for many items. The patchwork quilt was made not only for warmth but in order to utilize every last scrap of precious cloth. The earliest designs used many colors in tiny pieces, but as the settlers grew wealthier and had more leisure time, they could afford to plan their colors and patterns more elaborately. There were many types of crocheted and knitted edges. Incidentally, knitting is probably the oldest of all needlecrafts, dating back to the Egyptian pyramids!

The Mennonite German settlers who have mistakenly been labeled "Pennsylvania Dutch" came to the Colonies near the end of the century. They brought with them a peasant art that is quaint, colorful, and gay. They decorated their spice boxes, wood boxes, chests, cabinets, and other furniture with symbolic designs using the tulip, eagle, heart, tree, leaf, and various "hex signs." The reason the early settlers had so many boxes to decorate is that buffets, chests of drawers, bureaus, et cetera, as we know them today had not come into being yet. They had a dough box in the kitchen, a dower chest in the bedroom, a writing box on the table, and so on. These boxes later evolved into a kitchen cabinet, a chest of drawers, and a desk as people thought of putting legs on them.

By the end of the century, tea drinking was coming into vogue, and this in turn created a need for new household items such as teaspoons, tea tables, tea stands, and tea kettles.

The first beds were mostly low post or cupboard beds like those of Germany and Southern Europe. The later canopied beds and sleigh beds are often used with seventeenth-century style furnishings in many homes today. Other items which came later in history but which are commonly used with Early American furnishings today are candlewick bedcovers, needlepoint work, hooked rugs, and cross-stitch samplers. These were done only by aristocratic ladies at first; it was not until the early nineteenth century that they became widely popular.

The Pilgrims were somber and serious and even made a law that there should be no celebration of any kind at Christmas. Education was only for boys; the girls were expected to stay home and help with the work. The winters were cold and severe and life was difficult for grownups and children.

There are only a few dolls of this period in museums now, and it is unlikely that dollhouses were built in those early hard days. Those in Europe were of the cabinet type, and the wood was left natural inside and out.

CLARE'S EARLY AMERICAN DOLLHOUSE

Clare's Early American Dollhouse was built with birch wood and shellacked for a natural finish which is in keeping with actual seventeenth century dollhouses. The doors were cut horizontally so that each room has its own door. Strap hinges and door pulls of a colonial design add to the authenticity (Plate No. 15).

Plate 15.   Clare's Early American dollhouse was left natural and shellacked. The doors were cut horizontally to make four doors. Black strap hinges and door pulls are of a Colonial design. A small black eagle decorates the pediment.

[24]

Master Bedroom

The walls are a natural color burlap. The curtains are batiste. A stone fireplace is styrofoam covered with cloth in a stone design. Over the mantel are two pictures in brass curtain ring and rickrack frames. The hearth broom was made of an applicator stick and real broom straws. On the mantel is a tray purchased in an antique shop for 50 cents. The andirons are lamp finials. The wall shelf box is a push-out cigarette box and balsa wood. On the left is an imported "Indian" wall hanging with the tree-of-life design. It is actually muslin with outline and lazy daisy stitches. Two applicator sticks were used for dowels.

Clare's sister, Anne, wove the hearth rug on a pot-holder loom. The hooked rug beside the bed was really hooked. A crochet hook and yarn were used with burlap. The balsa wood, pencil, and pushpin night stand and the styrofoam, cardboard, and pencil field bed were inspired by those in the famous old Whipple House (1638) in Ipswich, Massachusetts. On the night stand is a toothpaste cap drinking glass, a souvenir pitcher from a vacation trip, and a wash bowl cut from a plastic cup. Below is a chamber vase made from a spray-can top, a curtain ring, and a large button for a lid. All are decorated with roses to co-ordinate the set.

The authentic bedcover is embroidered with crewelwork and lined with pink cotton flannel. The William and Mary desk was made with the grain bin pattern. It was made of a box, balsa wood, and beads. The laminated cardboard banister-back chair is authentic, even to its rush seat! The books are corrugated cardboard covered with magazine ads and colored paper. The candle holder is a bottle cap. The lantern hanging from the ceiling is a window shade pull and glows in the dark!

Nursery

The nursery walls are grooved and painted white to represent the old whitewashed walls popular late in the century. The curtains are natural colored broadcloth. The shelf holds a zipper case bandbox over a styrofoam and sandpaper mantel. The candle holders are birthday candle holders, upside down with the point cut off. The pewter tray is a cocoa box lid decorated with a decal. An early primitive portrait cut from a magazine is framed in a cardboard frame. On the right is a bed warming pan like that in the master bedroom. It is a pill bottle cap and applicator stick.

A spool lantern hangs from the ceiling. The imported rug is really a bandanna. The wing chair was once a quart milk carton. A night table of clothespins, styrofoam, and balsa wood holds a washbowl made from a plastic cup and a toy cream pitcher which belonged to a tea set too large for the dollhouse. The chamber vase is a spray paint can top. Flowers were cut from cloth and glued on to make a matched set.

[25]

The bed, a box with pencil posts and styrofoam canopy, is topped with a fishnet canopy cover made from a plastic doily. The quilt is patchwork patterned cotton lined with pink cotton flannel and machine quilted.

The wicker cradle was inspired by the one used by Peregrine White, one of the baby boys born on the Mayflower in 1620. It is a party favor basket with balsa wood rockers and cloth canopy. The wastebasket is a pill bottle, and the step stool is styrofoam and beads. The Pennsylvania Dutch dower chest is a painted recipe file box. The child's chair is made of popsicle (or paste) sticks and balsa wood.

Living Room

The living room walls are covered with gold colored burlap to give a homespun look. The ceiling has exposed beams made of window-shade sticks. The pewter chandelier is made with styrofoam and jewelry chains. The window shutters are balsa wood and part of a matchstick bamboo place mat. The curtains are batiste. The stone fireplace is styrofoam with stones cut from a cork placemat. The andirons are lamp finials, the Pennsylvania Dutch wood box is a bandage box. The candle holders were once earrings. A laminated cardboard picture frame holds a crewel embroidery. The sconces are balsa wood. A cocoa box top frames a portrait cut from a magazine. On the left is a wall shelf box made from a small box and balsa wood. The plate holder is a hairpin.

The corner cabinet is made of a cardboard box and balsa wood. Clare's sister, Elizabeth, crocheted the rug for her. The "Country Chippendale" wing chair is made of corrugated cardboard and clothespins. (This term is used by historians to describe some of the earliest wing chairs which were rustic in design and construction but were similiar in line to later ones.) Behind the chair is an end table of styrofoam, balsa wood, and spools. On it is a Bible-box which is an aspirin box painted black. The sawbuck table, made of balsa wood, holds a lamp which is a Christmas candle.

The modern wing back couch is a detergent box. The real afghan was crocheted by Clare's grandmother who made a "granny square"* and worked a border around it. A box top, styrofoam, and clothespins were used for the coffee table. The tray is a cocoa box lid. The roundabout or corner chair is laminated cardboard.
* A single section or square from an afghan pattern

Kitchen

The walls of the kitchen were left natural. Window shade sticks were used for the exposed beams. The window blind is part of a matchstick bamboo placemat. The wood fireplace has a movable crane made with coat hanger wire and cup hooks. The cooking pot is a ketchup bottle cap and a hairpin. On the mantel are jelly cups and canned cinnamon roll icing lids. The candle holders are birthday candle holders reversed. Over the fireplace is a rifle made of an applicator stick and balsa wood. The powder horn is a cap from a liquid sweetener bottle. The long-handled ladle is a spice spoon. The pot holder is felt. The bucket is a souvenir. The plate holder is a hairpin, and the pewter spoon rack is balsa wood. The trivets are cut from plastic doilies and sprayed black.

On the right is a balsa wood shelf. The pewter plates are the same as those on the mantel. The drinking beakers are toothpaste tube caps. The pheasant is made of real feathers and came from the dime store. The candle box on the right wall is a lipstick case held by cup hooks. (A box was necessary because the old candles were made of animal fat and had to be kept out of the reach of mice.) A balsa wood grain storage bin is most often full of sugar-coated cereal. The lid is hinged with cloth. The wrought-iron candle ceiling fixture is made of styrofoam, beads, and chains. The felt rug has an embroidered eagle on it. The ladder-back rocker is laminated cardboard with a rush seat of twine.

Styrofoam and beads made the stool. The Colonial table and bench are balsa wood and styrofoam. A handkerchief serves as a table cloth, removed here in order to show the table. The pewter plates are the same as the ones on the mantel, and the drinking beakers are sample lipstick cases. Clare's sister, Elizabeth, made the flower pot from a spray paint can top and plastic flowers. The Cromwellian chair is made of styrofoam and burlap with clothespin legs. The embroidery is crewelwork. The churn is a plastic medicine bottle and an applicator stick. The milk can in the corner is the salt container from a stove set for salt, pepper, and grease. The high chair is laminated cardboard.

[27]

5

A French Provincial and Late Colonial Dollhouse

EIGHTEENTH CENTURY DESIGN BACKGROUND

The eighteenth century was a time of elegance. Franklin, Washington, and Jefferson were helping to shape America's future, and Sir Christopher Wren was rebuilding London. Colleges were springing up all over the Colonies, and political independence was on everyone's mind. All this not only influenced our government but our arts and our home furnishings.

Colonial builders were copying Wren's Georgian style architecture, and the houses were getting larger and more expensive as dining rooms and drawing rooms were added. Interior woodwork was popular. Mantels were crowned with beautiful pediments, pilasters, and carvings, and windows and doors were framed with moldings. Some of this woodwork was simple and straight, while some was curved and decorated in the Louis XV manner popular in France. Instead of leaving the wood natural as they had in the seventeenth century, they often painted it white, cream, gray-blue, or green. Wallpapers were introduced during the first half of the century and were usually scenic or French-inspired patterns.

The new wealth of the century had created an interest in parlor games, dancing, and tea and coffee drinking, and therefore was to influence the taste in furnishings. The furniture was curved and decorative now and was beginning to be made in sets. Upholstery had been introduced, and furniture makers were anxious to use it. Chippendale was popular in England, and he, too, was inspired by the Louis XV style.

Clocks were made in Boston and Philadelphia early in the century. Glassmaking came to Pennsylvania a little later. Portrait paintings and cut silhouettes were created and sold by artists traveling on horseback. Because of the lack of professional training of these artists, these paintings have been referred to as "primitives." Silversmithing became a fine American art, and pewter, tin, and wrought iron were used for many things including chandeliers.

Hepplewhite was just one of many furniture makers to make the wing chair, present in almost every eighteenth century home. Draperies with valances and swags trimmed with elaborate fringes were imported from France. Fine china came from England. Many beautiful rugs were imported from Aubusson, France, and from the Orient.

The colonists were eager to follow the French styles of the time. In France, Marie Antoinette and Madame de Pompadour made powdered wigs popular and influenced colonial women's taste in many things. French women were beginning to be interested in flower arranging because of the beautiful Oriental vases and Dresden ceramics. This art eventually was taken up by American wives too.

The Rococo or Louis XV style of architecture and furniture was elaborate and used mostly in the grand palaces. The French people who lived in small villages all over France were as busy copying this elaborate style as the people in other parts of the world. They simplified the designs so that they were not only priced more reasonably but were more appealing. This simplified style eventually was known as French Provincial. It was sometimes painted in pale colors such as cream, white, and light green and was often gilded.

The French villagers not only simplified the furniture but the architecture as well. Checked marquetry and marble floors were used when they could afford them. They often panelled only one wall in a room. They even used the newly fashionable printed cottons and flocked wallpapers to fill in the center part of the wall panels to save on wood.

In the village of Jouy, France, Philippe Oberkampf established a cotton print factory. His cottons were less expensive than the elaborate silks and came to be in great demand. These toiles-de-Jouy cottons were used for draperies, wall coverings, and upholstery and were always one color on a cream ground. They were not only copied in the eighteenth century but are still much copied all over the world today!

In the American colonies petit point needlework was used for bedcovers and on furniture. Needlepoint was used for rugs, wall hangings, and upholstery. Some candlewick bedcovers were being designed by the aristocrats although they were not to become widely popular until the nineteenth century. Appliqué quilts were popular. Hooked rugs were beginning to be made, and these early ones were very similar to the needlepoint ones.

Pewter was often used instead of the more expensive silver in the smaller homes of the period, but when silver was owned, it was conspicuously displayed. Clocks, vases, and figurines were placed on the mantels as well as brass candlesticks. Brass fireplace accessories and embroidered fire screens were used. Sconces, table lamps, and crystal chandeliers not only gave light but added to the beauty of the rooms.

The formal dining table appeared during this period. Serving tables, candle stands, and game tables became popular also.

There are many superb houses of this eighteenth century style still standing all along our eastern shores today.

In this same century dollhouses were being made in Europe in the castles. The winters were long and grownups furnished them to pass the time away. Children were often only allowed to play with them on special occasions because they were so elaborate and costly. They were basically still the cabinet style with architectural features.

In America only a very few wealthy children owned dollhouses. Some of these can be seen in museums in the East today.

ANNE'S FRENCH PROVINCIAL DOLLHOUSE

Anne's French Provincial and Late Colonial Dollhouse is painted off-white on the exterior. It is trimmed with gold to resemble the Louis XV panelling. The folding doors take up little room and are thus well suited to corners and close areas. The handles are antiqued brass in a traditional style. See Plate No. 16.

Inside, the furniture is painted white to harmonize with the exterior. This was done for contrast with the other houses, and also to give a feeling that is associated with French furniture.

Master Bedroom

The walls have simple French Provincial panels of heavy cardboard glued onto them and painted with gloss enamel. (The Louis XV panelling used in the Victorian dining room can be used in this house as well. There was a nineteenth century revival of the period.) The lower part of the walls is covered with a quilted fabric to match the bedcover. The bead chandelier, the hairpin wall sconces, and the earring picture frames are typical of the period. The draperies are pink cotton satin with a matching valance trimmed with gold braid. The servant pull really rings. The Aubusson rug is a handkerchief.

Marie Antoinette's bed in the Petit Trianon Palace in France was the inspiration for the bed. It is upholstered styrofoam with bead feet. The quilted bedcover is the same fabric as the valance and on the walls. Canopied beds were commonly used in the American colonies, and both those used in the seventeenth century dollhouse are suitable for this house. The French ones are used here in order to give readers a wider choice of styles. The table is a wooden coaster on a laminated cardboard pedestal fashioned after Chippendale's famous pie-crust table. On it is a flower arrangement in a gold-decorated bottle cap.

[*30*]

Plate 16.   Anne's French Provincial dollhouse is painted off-white and trimmed with gold. The folding doors proved to be so functional that they were used as part of the basic cabinet design. The door pulls are antiqued brass in a traditional style.

The Louis XV side chair was made from a scouring powder can, and the vanity was made with styrofoam and cardboard. On it is a twentieth century lamp made of a cork, a doorstop, and a drawer pull. Hairpins and styrofoam were used for the vanity chair. The waste basket is a pill bottle, the washbowl is a cocoa box lid, and the drinking glass is a toothpaste tube cap. The bed warming pan is a modern woman's purse ash tray and sold in most gift stores. (The handmade type of warmer is seen in the nursery.)

Nursery

The nursery walls are covered in cotton percale to represent the toiles-de-Jouy fabrics. The ceiling border is gold and white braid. The main architectural feature of this room is the window treatment. The balsa wood shutters are painted off-white, incised, and trimmed in gold to represent molding. They are attached to the window facing with a cloth hinge so they really open and shut. The curtains are batiste. A

[*31*]

shelf of balsa wood and cardboard in a typical French Provincial design holds a bandbox which once contained a zipper.

The crystal and pewter chandelier is half a styrofoam ball, glitter, hairpins, and jewelry. The toiles-de-Jouy bed is a cigar box with pushpins for finials. A cradle made of laminated cardboard holds a baby. A rocker of authentic French Provincial design and the Chippendale table add elegance to the room. The peasant chair is laminated cardboard and clothespins. A table beside the bed is made of spools, a button, and styrofoam with cardboard. The lamp is a bottle with a nut cup shade. The diaper hamper is a bandage box, and the umbrella stand a pill bottle. The paper umbrellas are party favors.

Felt was embroidered for the needlepoint rugs. (These designs can be used for hooked rugs also. See needlework pages.) A picture on the left wall is framed in a piece of old jewelry. The "primitive" portrait was cut from a magazine and framed with laminated cardboard. A photograph of Anne is framed in a miniature frame, and on the right wall a cocoa box lid frames an embroidery. The child's chair is made with popsicle or paste sticks and balsa wood. The footstool is styrofoam covered with embroidered silk. Pushpins serve as feet.

Dining Room

The dining room walls are covered with a flocked gift-wrap paper and a mural cut from a magazine. The molding strip is balsa wood and the ceiling border is braid. The floor is made from vinyl tile which was heated in the oven and cut with scissors into 2″ squares. A crystal chandelier made from glass beads, styrofoam ball, jewelry, and hairpins and the wooden Georgian mantel make this the most architecturally authentic room in the house.

Balsa wood and cardboard decorated with cut-outs from plastic doilies make a corner cabinet which holds an assortment of miniatures. The canisters are vitamin sample bottles, and the silver trays are various flat lids. The Austrian shade is batiste. On the left is a compact mirror trimmed with gold braid and a patriotic sticker. The sconces are earring clips and necklace clasps. Below is a Louis XV style, Chippendale serving table trimmed with decals. The silver teapot is a small pepper shaker.

The dining table is styrofoam, spools, and a wooden coaster with a vinyl top. The table cloth is a handkerchief. The drinking beakers are sample lipstick cases. The napkins are 1½″ squares of batiste fringed on the edges. The red corduroy Empire chairs were made from quart milk cartons. The Napoleonic tree is a bottle cap and a styrofoam ball. The white Louis XVI chairs are laminated cardboard.

The candle holders on the mantel are chrome drawer pulls, and the pheasant came from the dime store. The fireplace fender was once a bracelet and the umbrella stand a plastic medicine bottle with eagle stickers glued onto it. The kitten is china.

Drawing Room

The drawing room walls are covered with mattress ticking to represent a later Empire period. The mantel with its pediment and molding is authentic Georgian. Red satin was used for the draperies which have tiny bone curtain rings. The large chandelier was made of old necklaces. On the mantel are brass candlesticks from a gift shop. (For the homemade type see dining room and other houses.) The flowers are in a vase that was once a part of a nail polish bottle. The andirons are lamp finials, and the brass wood basket was intended to hold cigarettes. A pill bottle cap, applicator stick, and cardboard make the embroidered fire screen.

The early nineteenth century banjo clock is a boy's toy watch and balsa wood with a piece of old jewelry for decoration. A patriotic sticker silhouette of George Washington hangs over the secretary. A portrait cut from a magazine in a cardboard frame is flanked by two flower prints in brass curtain ring frames. The needlepoint rug is felt with a wide floral braid border.

The styrofoam and velvet couch is Louis XVI. It has clothespin legs as does the Hepplewhite wing chair. The round throw pillow is a powder puff. The small lamp table, early Duncan Phyfe style, is made of laminated cardboard. On it is a souvenir cup and saucer on a stand.

A secretary of balsa wood with plastic doily cutouts for carving and a matching laminated cardboard chair are Chippendale. (Since Chippendale's early chairs were similiar to the Queen Anne style, this pattern can be used for either one.) The books are corrugated cardboard covered with paper. Magazine advertisements provided the jackets. The feather quill rests in a bead on a balsa wood base. A tiny letter, really written with the quill by Anne, says "I love you."

A Neo-Classic period coffee table is styrofoam, balsa wood, and pencils with a vinyl top and pushpin feet. (A simpler coffee table can be made with the CHIPPEN-DALE CHAIR pattern.) The candy dish is made of earrings and the fruit compote from a drawer pull and a large button.

The Louis XV end chair is laminated cardboard decorated with lace to resemble carving. The embroidered footstool is styrofoam and beads. Over the chair is a silhouette framed with a lid from a small zipper case.

6

A Nineteenth Century
Victorian Dollhouse

NINETEENTH CENTURY DESIGN BACKGROUND

After the Revolutionary war came the post-Colonial and Federal, and the American Eagle periods. The great Greek Revival period was in the first part of the nineteenth century.

Jefferson promoted a classical style based on the architecture of Greece and Rome. His Monticello was completed in 1809, and his wealthy neighbors began building in the same style with his advice. Federal furniture reflected the designs of Hepplewhite and Sheraton. Duncan Phyfe became famous for his Empire furniture at the beginning of the century.

Princess Victoria became Queen in 1837, and her long reign provided historians with the term "Victorian Era." During this era America changed from a rough agricultural country to one of the great industrial powers of the world. The period brought about important social changes such as the two-party system and the public school system. The telegraph, ocean steamer, sewing machine, gaslight, telephone, electric light, and photography were all invented during these important years.

The Greek Revival period stimulated interest in interpreting other historic periods in architecture, and was followed by Egyptian, Gothic, Oriental, Italian, Mansart, Romanesque influences, and finally by the Octagonal style. The Gothic style which was translated into stone and wood for country churches across the nation has become a symbol of rural America. Decorated with jigsaw cut wood trim it has also been called the "Gingerbread" style. Most of the old western towns are of the mansart type of architecture. The old false-front buildings, which sometimes had elaborate faces of wood made to imitate stone, were really little more than sheds behind. This western-type Victorian was homey, and the elaborate furniture was in strong contrast to the rough exterior.

Interiors were crammed and decorated to the last inch. Figured wallpapers, floral carpets, and potted plants were common to every room. The windows were huge and heavily draped with velvets and brocades. Cornices were commonly used, and brass, iron, and wood were some of the materials from which they were fashioned. Many mantels were small and made of marble while others imitated Tudor and Italian styles.

Overstuffed chairs, tufted ottomans, hassocks, and marble-topped tables became popular. Bentwood furniture became popular when Thonet began to bend wood under steam for curved and curled chairs and tables. John Wickersham manufactured iron furniture such as bedsteads, settees, chairs, washstands, tables, and hatstands. His architectural trim was used for fences, railings, gratings, balconies, mantels, and many other kinds of ironwork.

The black Hitchcock chairs belong to the early nineteenth century. They were inspired by those of Sheraton. The simple and functional Shaker furniture belongs to this period also. The Shaker rocker was often used on porches. The Boston rocker was commonly used throughout the century.

The invention of the coiled metal spring made plush, tufted upholstery popular. Antimacassars were used to protect the furniture from the hair oil which the men plastered on their hair. The oil was imported from the port town of Macassar; hence the name anti-Macassar. The outstanding styles of Victorian furniture are French Empire, Gothic, and Louis XV revival. The Louis XV styles were plush, heavily decorated interpretations of the originals. Probably the most famous furniture maker of the time was John Belter who copied these Louis XV designs and made them extremely popular. The dresser or bureau was introduced during this period and has been commonly used ever since.

Accessories such as statues, wax flowers, glass domes, shell work, gilt mirrors and frames, fringed cushions, petit point mottoes, cross-stitch samplers, whatnots loaded with bric-a-brac, and beadwork were everywhere. Currier and Ives colored lithographs were produced during this era. Later the daguerreotype process of photography made silhouettes and primitive portraits go out of style.

Aubusson rugs were still popular as well as Oriental rugs. Navajo rugs were popular in the West. The hooked rug, floral or scenic in design, became popular during the first half of the nineteenth century. Animal-skin rugs were used because of the popularity of big game hunting.

Candlewick bedcovers had been made by some aristocratic women in the eighteenth century but it was in the nineteenth century that they were made in great number. This style eventually became known as chenille when the loops were cut. "Chenille" is the French word meaning caterpillar!

[35]

Christmas as we celebrate it today was started when Prince Albert, a German, introduced the Chistmas tree to Queen Victoria and their family. This custom of decorating a tree quickly spread to America. It was not uncommon for little girls of this period to have dollhouses. They were mostly architectual and copied the various styles of real houses. There were some attempts to manufacture them, but they were for the most part still made by a local carpenter as in the past.

The homes of both Lincoln and Theodore Roosevelt are excellent examples of Victorian interiors. In the Lincoln room in the White House is a fine collection of this style also. General Grant's home is representative of a gaudy style known as the "General Grant style."

ELIZABETH'S VICTORIAN DOLLHOUSE

Elizabeth's nineteenth century dollhouse has painted architectural features. The windows, doors, and pediment are typical of many old Victorian town houses still standing. The house front was painted not only for variety but also because the doll-houses of the nineteenth century were architectural in design. White ceramic knobs were used so they would not distract from the painted features. Steps were added because they seemed natural. Plate No. 17.

Master Bedroom

The master bedroom walls are covered with a pillow case percale in a flower stripe design typical of the period. Because it is intended for pillow cases the ceiling border is matching. Styrofoam, hairpins, and jewelry were used for the chandelier. Taffeta and nylon draperies are crowned with a pierced brass cornice made of cardboard and plastic doily cutouts. The cord and tassel came from a perfume bottle. On the left, a lamp finial, hairpin, and earring make a gaslight. The picture was a gift to Elizabeth's father when he was three years old. A canned cinnamon roll icing lid frames a needlepoint embroidery. Over the bed hangs a real cross-stitched sampler which says "Bless Our Home." An oval of felt was embroidered and lace trimmed to become a hooked rug.

The ladies' chair was made from a scouring powder can and its little footstool is a rectangle of styrofoam with bead feet. The embroidery is one of those machine-made designs which can be found at most notion counters. The antimacassar is batiste and lace. The pot-bellied stove was made from a mustard jar.

The bureau is typical of Lincoln-style Victorian. It is laminated cardboard and a box with plastic doily cutouts, lace, and braid for carving. The wash bowl and pitcher set came from a gift store. (For homemade types, see Early American bedrooms.)

Plate 17.   Elizabeth's Victorian dollhouse has painted architectural features. White ceramic knobs were used to blend with the background. The door, windows, and pediment are painted with pink and two shades of gray. The steps are separate from the cabinet and can be moved around.

The bed is made of styrofoam and cardboard and matches the bureau. The bedcover is authentic candlewick with a crocheted edge. The throw pillow design matches the footstool, and the hatbox is a covered zipper case. The pill bottle vase holds plastic greenery. Corks and a toothpaste tube neck made a lamp which sits on a laminated cardboard Duncan Phyfe table. The hat stand is a pencil, nails, and nail polish bottle. The cowboy hat is a pencil sharpener with the works removed.

This ceiling and the others in this house have lacy gold decals to represent the old carved and embossed ceilings of the period.

Nursery

A rose print percale covers the walls. The border is a floral ribbon. The styrofoam and cardboard mantel is painted to look like marble. The fireplace fan is cardboard and part of a plastic doily, the clock is a toy watch and balsa wood. The gaslight chandelier is made of styrofoam, beads, and hairpins. The curtains are pink velvet and the valance of felt. The picture on the left wall is a Currier and Ives in a cardboard frame, the photograph is of Elizabeth in a miniature frame. The baby is a magazine picture in a cocoa box top. The mirror came from a compact. It is trimmed with braid. A ribbon holds two small flower pictures framed with curtain rings. The bearskin rug was made from an old piece of bunny fur. The bed is a box and two coat hangers. The comforter is lined with the same fabric as the wall and machine quilted. The table is styrofoam, spools, and a wooden button. A cheese box draped with batiste and lace serves as a bassinet. The little chair is a dime store pincushion. The table is styrofoam and hairpins. The dollhouse is part of a miniature imported farm set. The hip bath was cut from a plastic cup. The bath brush is a mascara brush.

The lamp is made of two fishing corks and the neck of a toothpaste tube. The shovel is balsa wood and a hairpin. The teddy bear, which was named for Teddy Roosevelt, is made of yarn. The rocker is laminated cardboard. The foot warmer is a match box and four beads.

Dining Room and Kitchen

The walls are paneled with cardboard moldings. An embroidered fabric looks like damask in the center of the panels. The floor is vinyl which resembles stone. The chandelier is styrofoam, beads, and hairpins. The cupboard was made from a soap box and balsa wood. It holds jelly-aspic molds, food made from styrofoam scraps and magazine ads, a miniature gelatin mold set, various types of tea sets, miniature foods and cleaners from toy sets, and canisters which held vitamin samples. The canisters now hold cookie decoration candies. There is also a dinner bell.

The Hitchcock chair is laminated cardboard. The china kitten peeps out of a birthday favor basket.

The table is styrofoam and cardboard. The table cloth is a handkerchief. The "crystal" candle holders are glass drawer pulls. The vase is a bottle cap and the drinking tumblers are sample lipstick cases. The 1½″ napkins are fringed batiste.

The chairs are laminated cardboard. A doll stand holds a bird cage window shade pull while a papier-maché bird sits on top. The pill bottle vase holds plastic flowers. Curtain rings serve as picture frames while a hairpin serves as a plate holder. The stove and the dry sink were both made of boxes. The trivets on the wall were cut from plastic doilies and painted black.

Parlor

The walls are covered with a flower-striped cotton. The ceiling border is lace in a swag design. The large chandelier is made of beads. The window is draped with batiste curtains and a green velvet swag. The authentic nineteenth century mantel is wood painted to look like marble. The andirons are lamp finials. The magazine basket is a novelty item for holding cigarettes. The "Ming" vases are plastic medicine bottles with painted trees, the glass dome once held a tooth brush, and the statues are a wooden bead and an animal which belongs to the same miniature set as the tiny doll house in the nursery. The trophy head was cut from a 5-cent plastic toy and mounted on a piece of cork. The sampler is really cross-stitched.

In the corner is a bric-a-brac shelf made of balsa wood. The pictures are sections from an old bracelet. The rug is a piece of tapestry cloth. The secretary is made from a cloth-covered box which is decorated with cutouts from plastic doilies for carving. The books are paper-covered cardboard. The bird feather quill rests in a bead. The Duncan Phyfe lyre-back chair is laminated cardboard with an embroidered velvet seat.

Green velvet matching the window swag covers the curved back sofa. The sofa is built of cardboard, styrofoam, and clothespins. The end tables are laminated cardboard and styrofoam. A doorstop topped with a styrofoam ball makes a lamp. The green chair is a salt box with plastic hairpin legs to resemble Thonet's bent wood furniture. A salt shaker tea pot sits on a cocoa-box-lid tray on the laminated cardboard coffee table. The fruit compote is a sewing machine bobbin and earring. The embroidered footstool is styrofoam and beads. The umbrella stand is a pill bottle and the antimacassars are batiste with crocheted edges. On the sofa is a 6″ square afghan which Elizabeth's grandmother crocheted. The floor lamp is a pencil and a cork. The base of it is a disk from a baby toy.

7

Needlework and Accessories

Of all the things that can be added to the dollhouse, none will increase its value, both in terms of sentiment and material worth, as much as the handmade needlework items. Even a dollhouse furnished with manufactured furniture and miniatures or an antique collection will need linens, rugs, and curtains. In the Warren dollhouse (plate No. 10) the fine carpet in the drawing room was worked by Mrs. Warren to represent accurately an Aubusson rug. In the same room, the center room on the right, is a fire screen which she embroidered. Her needlework not only increased the beauty and value of the house, but the items she made are valuable for their own sake.

The main reason miniature needlework is so much fun to do is that you can hook a rug in a few days, make a quilt in an evening, or fringe a set of dinner napkins in a matter of minutes! Many Scout and Campfire Girl leaders have found that the girls enjoy learning on miniature needlework projects because of this, and they have a toy when finished which makes it even more fun. The needlework designs shown in this book are all authentic, but they have been greatly simplified so that they can be worked by all age groups. The items can be added to the house over a period of months or years after the furniture is made.

Be sure to embroider your name or initials and the date somewhere on the piece before you finish. Think how precious it will be in just two or three years, and how much more precious it will be a generation from now! Those little cloth labels with names embroidered on them can be stitched on the undersides of the linens, but the date should be added.

The item which probably does more to set a mood and add warmth to a room than any other thing is the rug. It is one of the easiest items of all to make or to discover. First of all, I have worked out five authentic patterns which can be worked in petit point, embroidered, hooked, or even painted.

One of the simplest and most charming rugs which needs no pattern is the crocheted oval. Cotton rug yarn or wool yarn can be used. Multicolored yarn makes a brilliant "country" type rug. Just chain about ten stitches and then increase on the curves each time around.

Authentic rugs can be woven with yarn or rag strips on small pot holder looms, and the edges can be fringed. If you prefer knitting, there are many shapes and sizes of rugs to be made. Real braided rugs can be made of yarn.

The bedcover designs can be used for large rugs. These rugs as well as the bedcovers can be cut straight or scalloped on the edges. If a soft fabric is used, the rug should be lined. It can then be reversible. Felt can be used so that no hem or lining is necessary.

It isn't necessary to make rugs, however, because there are so many possibilities just waiting to be used. Handkerchiefs with borders make Aubusson and Oriental rugs. Bandannas can be used for Oriental rugs. If they are too large, make a tuck at the edge of the border on one side. When this is pressed and then placed to the rear of the room, it will not be noticed. Plastic doilies come in many sizes, shapes, and colors, and most of them are suitable for rugs. Their lacy delicate look is well scaled to the dollhouse. Place mats of all types are well suited although the woven ones are more expensive than the plastic ones.

Other things which can be used for rugs are washcloths, small guest towels, fabric, table napkins, old rugs or bath mats which can be cut up, small-size braided chair pads, small-size hooked chair pads, and even pot holders.

Curtains, as well as rugs, can help to give a room a mood and a period. Drapery panels should be about 15½" x 6". When used with sheer curtains, they can be about 3½" wide. Cottage curtains should be about 7" long. Use two small cup hooks for brackets. An applicator stick, pencil, plastic straw, dowel, or just a piece of paper rolled very tightly and glued can be used for rods. Beads can be put on the ends for decoration. Be sure to make the top hem to fit the rod you choose. The drapery pulls shown in the photographs are made of gold cord, fringed and knotted on the ends. Servant pulls can be made in the same manner. Austrian shades should be about 6" x 18".

The short swag in the Victorian parlor should be about 5½" wide x 14" long. Stitch and gather at an angle about 4½" from each end. Check the distance between hooks for this because it will vary. This type of swag can be full length. Make it about 5½" x 36".

A flat swag can be cut from felt and decorated with gold braid as in the Victorian nursery. Make it about 6" x 4". Fold and cut a scalloped swag shape. Hem top for rod.

Valances like that in the French Provincial bedroom can be made from a piece of fabric about 6″ x 8″. Fold it and sew in a scallop design. Leave an opening for turning. Trim with braid or fringe. Hem top. This and the felt swag can have a thread loop at each corner for the ends of the rod so they can be used on the same rod as the curtains. A ruffle or fringe can be used for valances and they require little or no sewing. Cardboard cornices can be made for a very formal look. Wood or balsa wood can be used too.

Tiny bone rings were used for the French Provincial drawing room draperies. The panels were pleated at each ring. Five rings were used for each panel. The rings are usually sold at the counter with knitting and crochet items. Large handkerchiefs can be used for curtains, and there is a lacy fabric sold for doilies which can be used without hemming. This fabric can be used for crocheted bedspreads too.

Of all the things you can make for a dollhouse, probably the articles that will be the most fun and create the most excitement from children and adults will be the bed linens. Dolls do not have to have them and a dollhouse can look finished without them, but you won't be able to resist making them . You have to pull the bedcover back to reveal the sheets, blankets, and pillowcases, and maybe that's part of the fun.

If bedcovers are lined, it is not only quicker than hemming them, but it is like making two at the same time because they can be turned over. There is no storage problem for that extra cover. The piece of fabric left over from the wall can be used for the lining for a coordinated room.

Some of the rug designs can be used for bedcovers, especially the embroidered eagle. The border design should follow the edge of the bedcover instead of being close to the eagle as it is on the rug pattern.

The small needlepoint and crewel designs used on stools, chairs, wall hangings, etc., can be used for bedcovers. Use fabric about 15″ x 9″. Draw first design in the center, then repeat, placing the designs about 1″ apart until cover is complete. A simple border can be added. The designs can be arranged in a checkerboard pattern. Two different designs can be alternated. There are many combinations and arrangements which can be used. For ideas, look at pictures of quilts in magazines and catalogues.

The "Tree of Life" wall hanging can be used for a rug or for the center on a bedcover.

The design for the candlewick bedcover can be used for appliqué. When this is done, it can be simplified slightly by eliminating the lines which join the flowers in the center and the dots. Draw the design on the back of the bedcover. Lay this down on the cloth to be used for the appliqué. This fabric should have the right side down. Stitch around the lines with a very small stitch. Trim away cloth very close to the stitches, then buttonhole stitch around the design on the right side by hand or automatic machine. Many of the stencil designs can be used for embroidered or appliquéd bedcovers in the same manner as the small needlepoint and crewel designs already described.

Small checked gingham can be cross-stitched for clever bedcovers. This is an easy method for beginners. There are many printed patterns available in stores for this. Your own original designs can be worked out on the back side with a pencil. Also, there are pillowcase border designs which can be purchased and used for bedcovers, rug borders, and other dollhouse items. Gingham smocking can be used also.

There are many knitting and crochet patterns which can be used, at least in part, for dollhouse needlework. Table and bed linens, antimacassars, rugs, afghans, and other things can be made from all or part of items described in needlework books. Sometimes just the center part of a bedspread, afghan, or tablecloth section can be used for a miniature. Make your sections about 2″ square. A simple way for a beginner to start is to crochet a plain circle or square and join them in one of many ways. Small cotton thread works best but yarn can be used also. The shaded, colored thread makes an interesting pattern. Crochet a lacy edge or sew on lace or fringe when completed. A miniature afghan is just about the size of one section from a full-size afghan. My daughters talked their grandmother into using "granny squares" and adding a crocheted border for theirs.

Miniature blankets can be crocheted, knitted, or made of wool or cotton flannel. A 1″ wide satin ribbon binding can be used so that it looks amazingly realistic.

Batiste, lawn, and percale work best for sheets and pillowcases. Lace or braid borders can be sewn on. They can be monogrammed. Almost any plain or print fabric can be used for mattresses and pillows. Make them to fit the bed, and tuft the mattress to keep it flat. Foam rubber, foam plastic, cotton, folded facial tissues, cloth, old stockings, and many other materials can be used for stuffing.

Things that are difficult for the beginner to hem, such as tiny 1½″ square batiste napkins or antimacassars, can be fringed on the edges. A more experienced person can not only crochet edges or whip on lace or tatting, but can even monogram them with a single strand of thread. This kind of detail is often found in antique dollhouses. Remember that anything you have in your own house can be made in miniature for your dollhouse with a little patience and imagination.

ACCESSORIES

Even more than furniture, miniature household implements represent a time in history. Look in our own homes today. We copy furniture from the past but our kitchen tools, telephones, appliances, etc. for the most part are strictly twentieth century. If a few hundred years from now a historian could see your home as it is today, how would he know it was a twentieth century home when the house and all the furniture are antiques or reproductions? He would know by the implements of everyday use. No matter how much we like antiques, we do not go back to the hard crude ways of getting our work done with the tools of the past.

A historian seeing a dollhouse can tell much about it from the many miniatures in it. Note the fabulous miniatures in the Nuremburg kitchen, plate No. 5. Remember the toy stoves, telephones, irons, etc. played with a generation ago? Remember how they were just like mother's at the time? Look at the many miniatures which come with the doll clothes today. All are up-to-date in design. Notice too, by the way, that people usually ask for the "dress that has the typewriter with it," or the "skirt that has a camera with it." Manufacturers are aware of the fact that the miniature pieces of equipment or accessories are often more sought after than the clothes. When these modern miniatures are put into the dollhouse, they are representing the time in which the owner collects them. "Grandmother Stover" and "My Merry" miniatures are excellent and plentiful as well as those made by the doll companies.

Almost everyone who starts a dollhouse at first wonders where to look for miniatures. After a while it becomes clear that they are all around us everywhere we go! When I look back now to those early days, I can't believe that I could have been so blind. At first I consciously searched for miniatures in places where I expected to discover them, then gradually my mind and my eyes became so accustomed to them that now miniatures seem to jump out at me from high shelves or from the midst of cluttered shop windows.

Naturally, the most obvious place to start looking is in toy stores, but they are not always the best source. During the past two years I have found some of our most interesting miniatures in museum souvenir shops, greeting card, party, and gift shops, restaurants, hotels, jewelry stores, novelty and costume shops, florist shops, dime stores, drugstores, book stores, baby and children's clothing stores, craft and hobby shops, and even grocery stores. One bit of advice to remember in all these places is that you must browse and look for yourself. Most often if you enter the store and ask for dollhouse miniatures, you will be told that they don't carry them! After you have looked at or purchased at least three marvelous items, the proprietor or sales person will exclaim, "Why, I never thought of that in terms of dollhouses!" One amazed shop owner I know plans to advertise dollhouse accessories next year because we discovered in her shop over twenty perfect ones which she had stocked without once thinking of selling them for this purpose.

Don't forget to look in souvenir shops and antique shops while vacationing. There are many charming miniatures perfectly scaled to the dollhouse which can be bought for only a few cents. Instead of the usual vacation junk which is forgotten in a few days, these worthwhile miniatures can be added to the dollhouse and become treasured keepsakes for years to come. The collecting will become a family interest, and the dollhouse will not only increase in sentimental value but also in historical value.

Be sure to frame a little picture of the owner of the house and be sure to date it for posterity. Since both the house and the furniture were designed to last for generations, take time to enjoy the creation of them. It will be a rewarding experience for all age groups. The house will become a kind of showcase for treasured miniatures, each of which will have its own meaning in the years to come.

There are many miniature household items which are difficult or impossible to locate, so I began to experiment with odds and ends around the house. I discovered that modern lids, packages, and containers could be used for almost anything from candle holders to cooking pots and pans. It would be impossible to show all the things my daughters and I thought of, but I did select some of those made of the things most commonly found in our homes today. With modern packaging changing every day, there will be new ideas for the miniatures every day. I hope the ideas shown on the accessories pages will merely stimulate you to look around and let your imagination go!

8

Kitchens, Commercially Manufactured Doll Furniture, Novelties, and Books

KITCHEN

The kitchen has always been a favorite of dollhouse enthusiasts of all ages from the early German kitchens to our present-day automatic plastic kitchen sets. I have worked out patterns for cooking fireplaces, wood stove, and a dry sink, but for readers who prefer the commercially manufactured kitchen equipment, there are many sets available. There is a very complete modern automatic kitchen perfect in scale which has food, dishes, and all necessary equipment. (Plate No. 18)

There is a metal kitchen set which is all built-in and is about 23″ long. It is complete and modern, but if you use it in the dollhouse, either remove the end cabinet or move the center partition of the dollhouse over when building it. Several mail order catalogues carry a less expensive metal set which is about 21″ and would require the same alterations.

Many toy and dime stores offer plastic kitchen appliances which can be purchased separately. There are about five units in all, and each has its own plastic miniatures. This type is very inexpensive but well designed and perfectly scaled. (Plate No. 19)

There are iron cook stoves available in novelty stores, gift houses, and a few toy stores. They are often advertised in popular magazines too. They are authentic and charming, and some include a coal scuttle and pans. Be sure to check the scale because they come in a variety of sizes. Get the size which has the cooking surface about 5″ from the floor. This is ever so slightly small for the 12″ dolls but the next size larger is too large, especially in depth. (Plate No. 20)

[*46*]

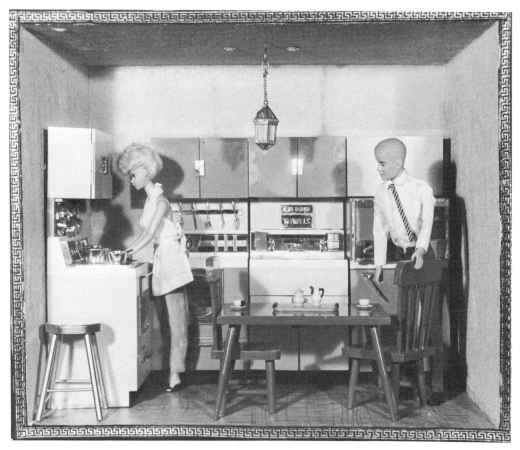

Plate 18.   A plastic kitchen with automatic appliances and complete supply
of utensils and equipment can be purchased in some toy stores.

Commercially Manufactured Doll Furniture

Most toy stores carry doll furniture which is the perfect scale for the dollhouses.
There are a number of companies who manufacture furniture, and most of it is sturdy
and in good taste. Do remember that there is a line of furniture made just for the 7″
and 8″ dolls which is too small for the 12″ dolls and can easily be confused with the
slightly larger scale. This smaller type fits the dollhouse beautifully, however, if it is
used exclusively. In fact, the tiny furniture can be used in the basic cabinet if the doors,
windows, and mantels are scaled down to it. I have met several collectors who already
had valuable collections of the 1″ to 1′ scale furniture who were interested in display-
ing it in a cabinet-type house.

I have seen very inexpensive plastic furniture which fits the dollhouse sold in dime

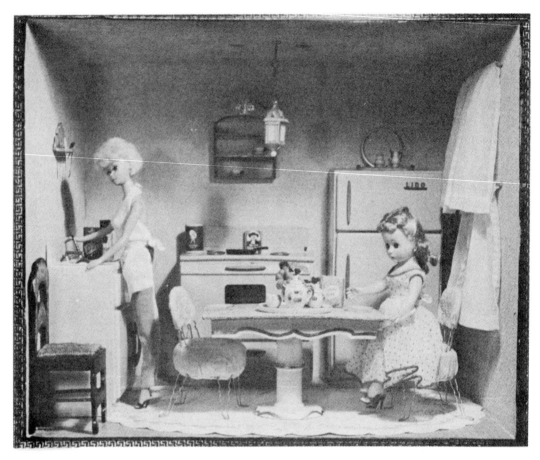

Plate 19.   Inexpensive plastic appliances can be purchased in many dime stores and toy shops. The units can be bought separately and come equipped with plastic utensils and food.

and variety stores. The designs were good and the plastic soft and permanent. It often comes in rather gay colors though. This kind is especially well suited to very young dollhouse owners who may be a bit rough on fine furniture.

There is a mail order house in California which carries a line of authentic antique-type doll furniture in three scales. F.A.O. Schwarz has dollhouses and furniture in their catalogue. Sears usually has kitchens and some furniture.

Some mountain souvenir shops carry charming country-type wooden doll furniture. As this usually varies in scale, it is a good idea to check the measurements to see if it is approximately a 2″ to 1′ scale.

Some of the doll makers put out a line of furniture made especially for their dolls.

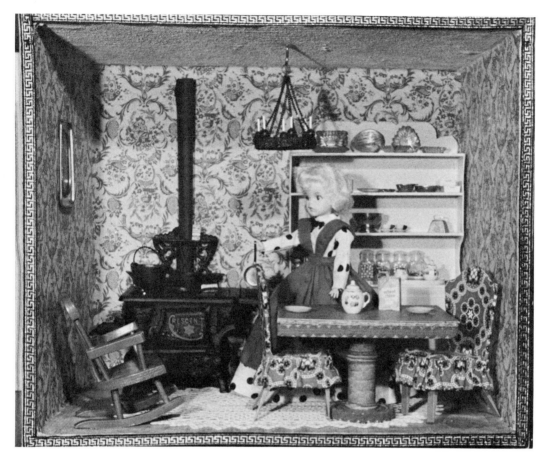

Plate 20.   An iron cooking range can be found in some novelty and gift stores and a few toy stores. It is authentic and has movable parts. The size shown here has the cooking surface about 5″ from the floor.

Occasionally, that made for the 12″ dolls is much too large for the house and the smaller dolls. Some of it is approximately 2″ to 1′ scale and can be mixed with that made with my patterns. It doesn't seem sensible to make furniture specifically for an 8″ doll or for a 12″ doll when the 2″ to 1′ scale is easier mathematically and at the same time can be used for both sizes and all those in between!

It is difficult to be specific concerning manufactured doll furniture because much of it is changing all the time, with new brands coming into the market and others which I can no longer locate. Plenty is available to be discovered with a little browsing and measuring. You won't need to measure after you become accustomed to the scale. Unfortunately, store clerks cannot always tell you the scale.

[*49*]

There are many novelty items which fit the dollhouses perfectly though they were never intended to be used as toys or in any way connected with dollhouses. One of the best sources of this type is mail order catalogues. The large catalogues often have a few things, but those small gift house catalogues are often full of them.

One of the cleverest items I discovered in more than one catalogue is a wooden recipe file box made to look like a kitchen cupboard! There are also tie racks with little drawers for cuff links, small spice cabinets, book ends, jewelry boxes, cigarette boxes, pipe racks, mirrors, banks, and many other items which imitate real furniture and are scaled just right. There is even a cigarette lighter in the shape of a pot-bellied stove and a planter shaped like a spinning wheel.

The novelty bric-a-brac items in the shape of everyday household items for dollhouses are proof of what we all already knew . . . that adults buy and enjoy miniatures all the time. I have seen pincushions which were Rococo vanity stools, chairs, foot stools, and wheelbarrows. There are lovely pill boxes in a large price range and music boxes shaped like everything from baby grand pianos to trunks. Miniature brass picture frames come in a variety of sizes and prices. One catalogue recently showed an "ash can" ash tray which is the most perfect trash can you can imagine. It even has a lid and handles. There are other ash trays which can be used for various dollhouse furnishings also.

The jewelry section of catalogues as well as stores should always be scanned by the miniature collector. Brooches make beautiful picture frames. When earrings and pins are the cameo type, they can be used just as they are. Any piece of jewelry with a stone can be used for a picture frame. Just pry out the stone, remove the clip, and glue in a small picture. Inexpensive dangle bracelets and necklaces often have fobs perfect for chandeliers, finials, statues for mantels and shelves, clocks, or bedposts. There are clear glass and plastic beads for crystal chandeliers. For a really fabulous chandelier, you can splurge and buy the iridescent crystal beads. There are necklaces made of several chains which will make all the chandeliers for a whole house. Once I bought a yard of chain at 30 cents a foot in an art store. A few days later I discovered, in a variety store, a long necklace made of six chains with a fob hanging on it for just 89 cents. It had several times as much chain with a fancy gold ball which could be a chandelier just as it was!

In one kitchenware department I discovered a set of measuring spoons shaped like miniature pots and pans and a set of aspic molds and cutters which are perfect cooky cutters and gelatin molds in the dollhouse.

I have one catalogue from a supplier of baking, cake decorating equipment, and party novelties. In it are dozens of miniature items such as tiny baskets, straw hats, hat boxes, cornucopias, umbrellas, Bibles, loving cups, miniature encyclopedias, birds, sprinklers, flower pots, chenille animals, lace fans, ice skates, wire chairs, and musical instruments. There are also records, bowling balls and pins, ping-pong sets, telephones, beer mugs, cigarette lighters, tools, eyeglasses, cameras, food, soda pop bottles, guns, and many more items. Most of them are meant to be used on cakes as decoration, and are only a few cents apiece.

Readers who may be interested in getting together in a group for the purpose of sharing ideas and enjoying the company of others with similar interests may join a chapter of the Doll House Clubs of America, or form their own group. The organization publishes a magazine with patterns, ideas, helpful information about miniatures, and with columns in which members can exchange and share ideas. It is a nonprofit organization founded for the educational and cultural purposes of fostering and promoting the decoration, furnishing and development of dollhouses. For those readers whose interests lean more toward dolls than dollhouses there is the Federated Doll Clubs of America. These groups are interested in the history and collection of antique and/or foreign dolls. They too have their own publication.

There are many books about dollhouses which you will want to read now that you have become exposed to the lifelong habit of collecting. Story books about miniature people or animals are absolutely wonderful reading for all ages. Of course, one cannot become interested in dollhouses without wanting eventually to know more about dolls too; some of them are on the book list also. I have listed some of the furniture and history books which I used for reference for my furniture designs to help you with your own original dollhouse furniture which you are bound to try sooner or later. These can be used as excellent reference books when planning your own home decorating as well as for dollhouses. You can even decorate a dollhouse room in the style and colors you plan to try in your own home and find out if you like it—like making a designer's model!

There are many good books concerning dollhouses which you will discover in book stores and libraries. The following list is not intended to be complete. It is a short list of the books which are favorites of mine and my daughters.

STORY BOOKS

Hans Christian Andersen, THUMBELINA, Charles Scribner's Sons
   (Illustrated by Adrienne Adams)
Mary Norton, THE BORROWERS, Harcourt, Brace & World
Beatrix Potter, THE TALE OF TWO BAD MICE, Warne.
Tasha Tudor, THE DOLLS' CHRISTMAS, Henry F. Walck, Inc.

BOOKS ABOUT DOLLS

Eleanor St. George, DOLLS OF THREE CENTURIES, Scribner
Eleanor St. George, DOLLS OF YESTERDAY, Scribner
Esther Singleton, DOLLS, Hobby House

DECORATING AND HISTORY BOOKS

Erwin Christensen, THE INDEX OF AMERICAN DESIGN, Macmillan.
Helen Comstock, AMERICAN FURNITURE, Viking Press.
Carl Drepperd, PIONEER AMERICA, ITS FIRST THREE CENTURIES, Doubleday.
Lester Margon, MASTERPIECES OF AMERICAN FURNITURE, Architectural Book Publishing Co.
Dorothy and Richard Pratt, A TREASURY OF EARLY AMERICAN HOMES, Hawthorn.
Sherrill Whiton, ELEMENTS OF INTERIOR DESIGN AND DECORATION, Lippincott.

BOOKS ABOUT DOLLHOUSES

Vivien Greene, ENGLISH DOLL'S HOUSES OF THE EIGHTEENTH AND NINETEENTH CENTURIES, Batsford.
Flora Gill Jacobs, A HISTORY OF DOLL HOUSES, Scribner
Audrey Johnson, HOW TO MAKE DOLL'S HOUSES, Branford.

Patterns For Dolls' Furniture, Dollhouse Plans, Needlework and Accessories

BASIC DOLLHOUSE CABINET PLANS AND BILL OF MATERIALS

Materials needed:
Two sheets of one-half inch plywood
Four pair of hinges (2 pair butt. and 2 pair folding screen)
One pair of latches
One pair of pull knobs
Finishing nails, wood glue, sandpaper, finishing materials

Optional items:
Cabinet lock with key
Four furniture legs

Bill of materials:

Description	Thickness	Width in inches	Length* in inches	Special cuts required
Two ends	all ½ inch plywood	15	$37\frac{1}{2}$	dado, rabbet, gain for hinges
One top		15	41	dado, rabbet
One bottom		15	41	dado, rabbet
Two center walls		$14\frac{1}{2}$	$16\frac{3}{8}$	door cut-outs
One floor		$14\frac{1}{2}$	41	dado
One back		41	$37\frac{1}{4}$	window cut-outs
One pediment		6	$41\frac{1}{2}$	angle cut
One base front		4	$40\frac{1}{2}$	----------
Four doors		$10\frac{3}{8}$	33	gain for hinges

*measure length to run with grain of wood

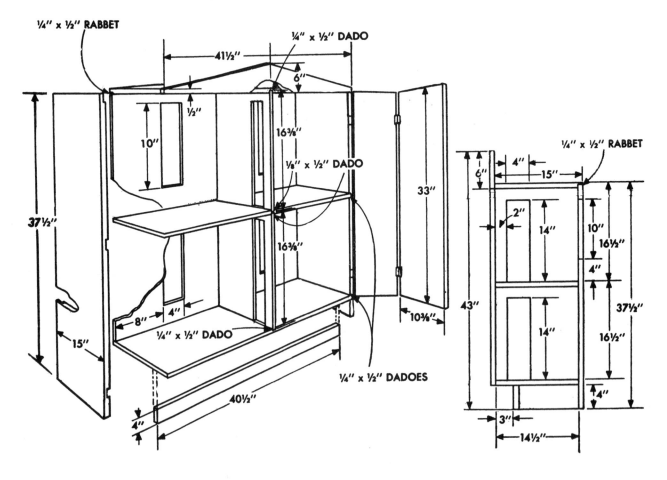

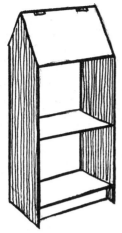

LEFT: A charming and economical variation of the basic cabinet is this two room with attic type. It has only one room less than the large cabinet but it needs only half the floor space! The attic should measure about 13" at the peak. The roof can be hinged. A dormer window can be built into the roof for an architectural house.

RIGHT: This style attic should also measure about 13" at the peak. When two of these cabinets are used together, there are six rooms! When architectural features are painted or built on the exterior they have the appearance of a row of town houses. The front panel can be held in place by spring type cabinet fastners.

ABOVE: The basic four room cabinet can have an attic room built onto it. If doors are used they can be cut to cover the attic room also. A separate removable panel can be used for the attic room instead. Any type doors can be used or it can be left open as pictured.

BELOW: For a really deluxe six-room house make the basic cabinet three rooms high. Any type doors can be used. These fabric panel doors are now available in most mail order catalogues. The fabric can match the room's color scheme for a really coordinated look! Since this will be rather heavy to move, casters can be added.

BELOW: Several rooms can be used horizontally for a formal cabinet. Legs can be purchased in most furniture styles. A separate table can be made for the cabinet to rest on, if preferred. The center room should have a panel which can be removed so there will be no door to be in the way of the other rooms. The end doors should be both right and left doors to open away from the middle.

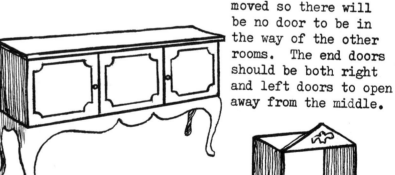

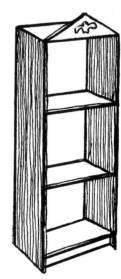

RIGHT: The cabinet can be three rooms high but only one room wide when floor space is at a minimum. Any type base and doors can be used. Any of the three-room styles can have all the rooms a doll will need if the kitchen and dining room are combined. This will leave the other rooms for parlor and bedroom.

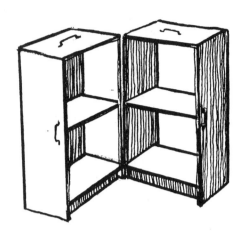

RIGHT: Louvered doors can be used. They can be purchased from most mail order catalogues, lumber yards, and department stores. Drawers can be installed for storage and casters and handles will make it easy to move about. If the pediment is left off, the cabinet will look like a piece of furniture.

ABOVE: This steamer trunk style cabinet solves the storage problem. It also is very convenient to work or play with because the units can be pulled in close to you on each side. Drawers can be installed in the bases. Be sure to use plenty of handles to make the design fully functional.

LEFT: If you wish to display a collection, build a formal cabinet with glass doors. The pediment is cut in a classic shape and legs are used to raise it up off the floor. The base can be built right onto the cabinet or it can be a separate table. Furniture legs can be found in any height so that the cabinet can be custom made to suit the owner.

LEFT: This display case provides space for showing a doll or miniature collection. Glass doors can be used on all surfaces or only on part of them. The cabinet can be raised up on legs or on a table. It can be made in three separate units so it will be easy to move or rearrange.

RIGHT: This cabinet has six rooms but seems much smaller than the one which is six full rooms because of the slanted roof. The attic can be just one large room if preferred. The cabinet can be architectural or plain with any kind of doors. The drawers can be used for extra miniatures or for dolls and doll clothes. Small wood mouldings can be used around the floors and ceilings for an elegant architectural interior.

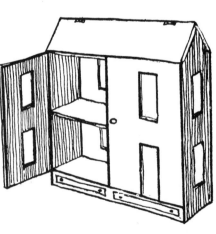

ABOVE: This house with glass doors and a drawer unit below is ideal for the collector. It provides plenty of storage and lifts the dollhouse up to adult eye level. This style goes well with living or dining room furnishings so it can be shared with guests at any time.

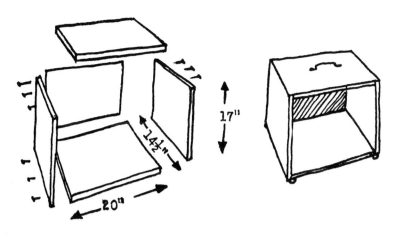

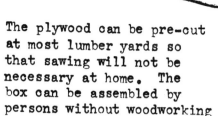

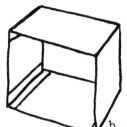

The plywood can be pre-cut at most lumber yards so that sawing will not be necessary at home. The box can be assembled by persons without woodworking experience.

PORTABLE ROOM (WOOD)

Use $\frac{1}{2}$" plywood, Cut top and bottom pieces 20" X 14$\frac{1}{2}$". Cut two side pieces 17" X 14$\frac{1}{2}$". Cut back piece 21" X 17". Assemble as indicated with small nails and glue. Put on back piece last. Use a large size drawer pull for carrying. Place handle about $\frac{1}{2}$" closer to the front than the back so box will tilt back just slightly when lifted. Four furniture glides or rubber bumpers can be put on the bottom to protect furniture. They also will hold the box above the drawer pull (the swinging kind) of the box below when two or more boxes are stacked. Doors can be added if desired.

PORTABLE ROOM (CORRUGATED CARDBOARD)

The cardboard can be cut from two large corrugated cardboard boxes such as those used for shipping soap, tissue, etc.. The cloth strips can be torn from muslin or old sheets. Use white liquid glue and brush on.

1. Cut two side pieces 14" X 16". Cut top and bottom pieces 20" X 14". Cut back piece 20" X 16".
2. Lay top, side, bottom, and side pieces out flat, as indicated in step a.
3. Glue cloth strips (about 4" wide) to each joint including half the fourth joint which will be joined later. Be sure to brush the glue on the cardboard, not on the cloth. Let dry for at least a half hour.
4. Fold around to join fourth joint. Fold so that cloth strips are on the INSIDE. It will help to support the box against something at this stage.
5. Glue back piece on with cloth strips.
6. Cover rest of joints now so that all joints are covered both on the inside and outside. Take each strip all the way to the edges so that each corner will have overlapping layers. This adds to the strength.
7. Cover outside of box with cloth. Use about 1$\frac{1}{2}$ yards of a sturdy cloth such as denim or corduroy. Bring cloth over the front edges of the box and into the inside for about an inch, as shown in step e.
8. Cover ceiling first, then walls, then floor. If fabric needs to be pieced, do this at a corner. Fold under the front edge, (or use the selvage edge) to give a finished look, as shown in step f. Floor can be carpeted with old rug, bath mat, terry cloth, etc.. A brown cloth can be used to give the look of a wood floor if small rugs are preferred. Vinyl or mosaic tile can be used also. Adhesive papers will not add to the strength of the box and are not recommended here.
9. A handle can be added if a small wood or metal piece is used inside to prevent screws from pulling through. This piece also provides a place for a hook for a chandelier.

Strap handles can be made from old plastic or leather belts.

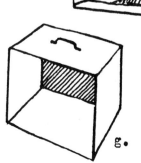

[57]

BELOW: The portable room becomes
a two-room house when an attic
is added. Make the attic about
13" high at the center point.
The doors can be cut to fit
the entire front or a separate
panel can be used for the
attic room. Handles can be
added to facilitate moving.

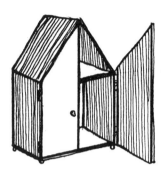

ABOVE: The box becomes a store
when a piece of wood is added
on top. The doors and windows
can be painted or actually
constructed. The Victorian
exterior patterns can be used
for these.

ABOVE: This style attic can be
hinged at the roof peak. The
box can be plain or architectural.
A dormer window can be built into
the roof and the front door can be
hinged to really open. This style
attic should measure about 13"
at the peak also.

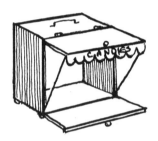

BELOW: Many old
cabinets can be used
for a dollhouse so
that no building is
necessary. This old
record cabinet was
discovered at an auction
for only a few dollars.
When the partitions
were removed there were
two rooms just slightly
larger than the 14" X
20" X 16" proportions
used in the house plans.
When painted or polished
this type can be used
in a dining or living
room so it can easily be
shown to friends.

ABOVE: If the doors are cut horizontally, the top one can become
a store canopy. This upper door can also become a false front for
a western type store when placed upright. Use small dowels to hold
the door in place as indicated. This style house is particularly
well suited for small boys. Any type store or building from a fort
to a grocery store can easily be made. It can be neatly closed with
all the miniatures safe inside.

LEFT: A small table can be
made to fit the box. The
box just happens to be about
the size of a small standard
end table and probably will
fit one you already have if
you prefer not to build one.
A table such as this one will
put the box at just the
right level for placing
beside a bed or chair.
This is particularly nice
if the owner is confined to
bed during illness.

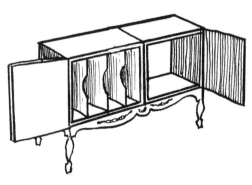

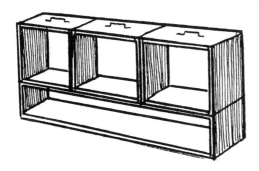

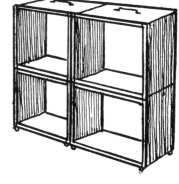

ABOVE: The rooms can be built into a bookcase unit or they can be built to sit on a unit made for them. Toys, books, collections, etc. can be stored on the shelf. If doors are used make the left one open to the left, the middle one a removable panel and the right one a right hand door.

ABOVE: When four units are stacked in this manner they make up a group that is similiar to the basic four room cabinet house. Several children can share this type and yet each can enjoy individual ownership at the same time by possessing a particular room.

RIGHT: If doors are used on a group of four or more individual rooms, be sure to plan the doors so that there will be both right and left ones. All the boxes can have handles for carrying.

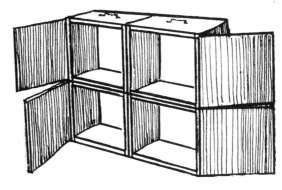

BELOW: The rooms can be built into a desk. The unit can have doors or be left open. This type can be a space saver since it is actually a desk and a dollhouse all in one. This type bookcase doll-house can actually be built right into a room for a modern "built in" wall. This unit can be built into a closet wall so that the desk, dollhouse, and storage units are all on one wall.

ABOVE: If an attic room unit is made and stacked on top of either one or two box units it won't be as tall as three full boxes but will actually have as many rooms. Doors and windows can be painted or built on the exterior. Make the attic room about 13" high at the peak, inside. Hinge the attic at the top.

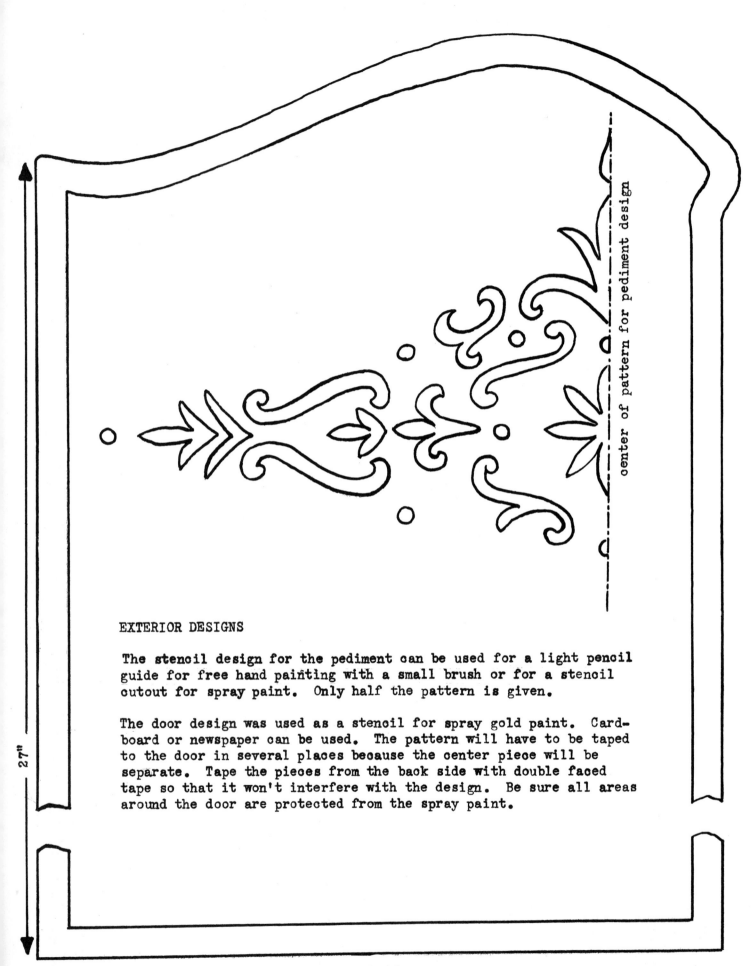

center of pattern for pediment design

27"

EXTERIOR DESIGNS

The stencil design for the pediment can be used for a light pencil guide for free hand painting with a small brush or for a stencil cutout for spray paint. Only half the pattern is given.

The door design was used as a stencil for spray gold paint. Cardboard or newspaper can be used. The pattern will have to be taped to the door in several places because the center piece will be separate. Tape the pieces from the back side with double faced tape so that it won't interfere with the design. Be sure all areas around the door are protected from the spray paint.

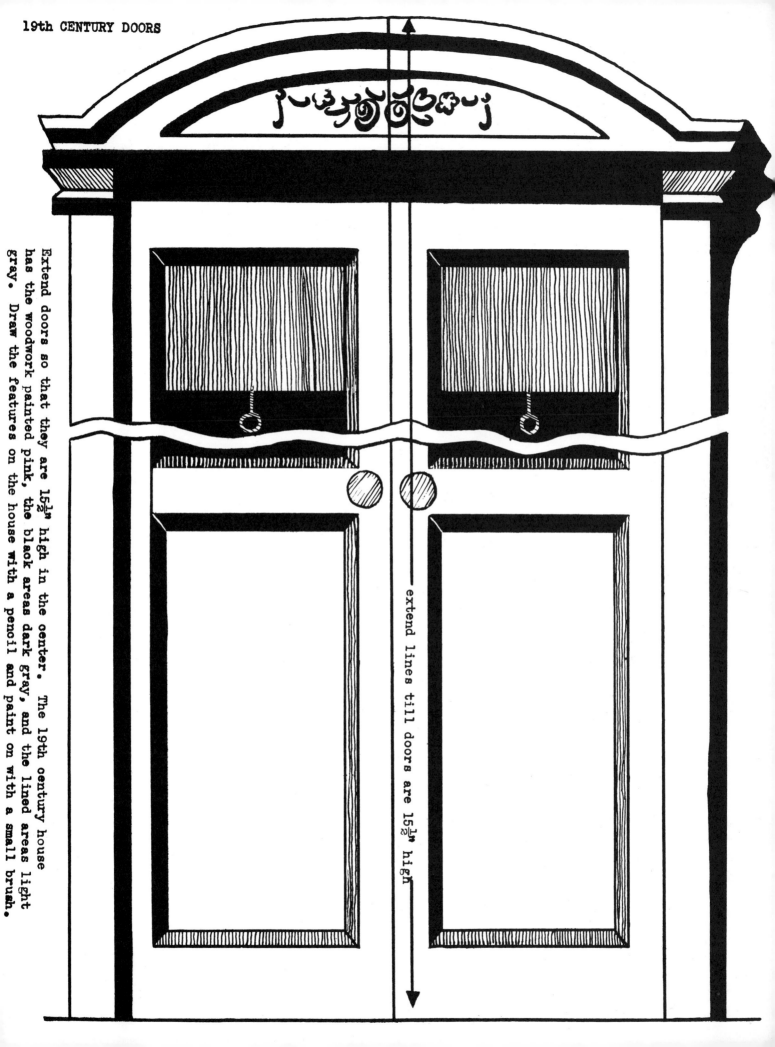

Extend doors so that they are 15½" high in the center. The 19th century house has the woodwork painted pink, the black areas dark gray, and the lined areas light gray. Draw the features on the house with a pencil and paint on with a small brush.

extend lines till doors are 15½" high

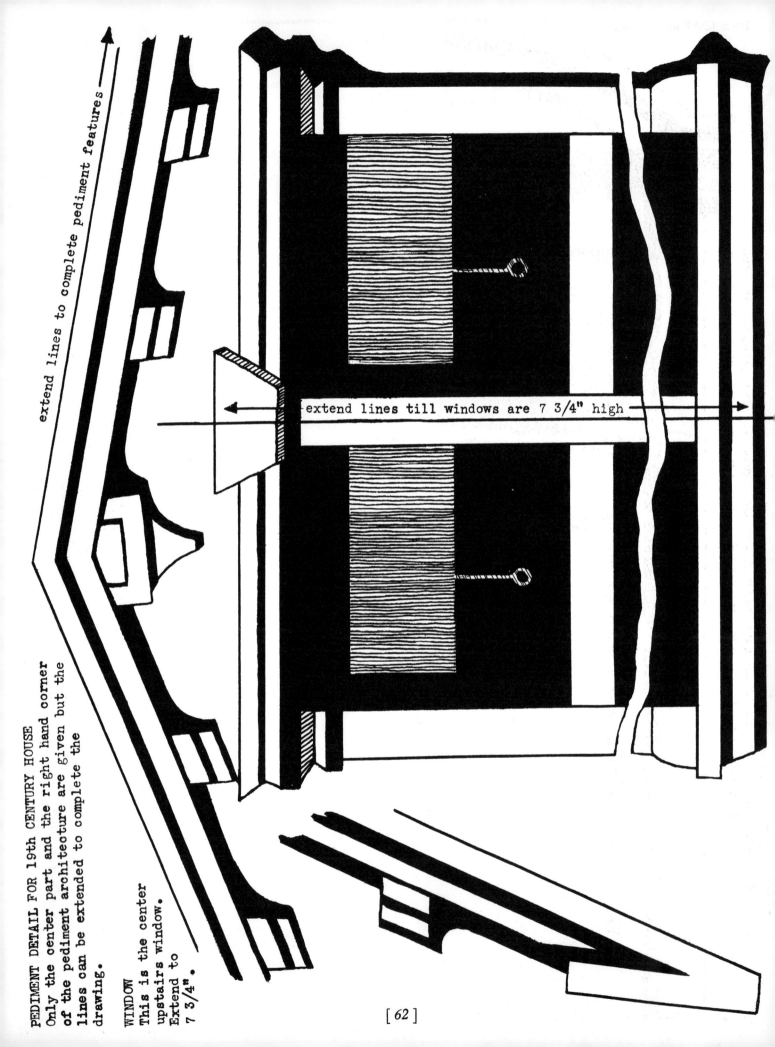

extend lines to complete pediment features →

PEDIMENT DETAIL FOR 19th CENTURY HOUSE
Only the center part and the right hand corner
of the pediment architecture are given but the
lines can be extended to complete the
drawing.

WINDOW
This is the center
upstairs window.
Extend to
7 3/4".

extend lines till windows are 7 3/4" high

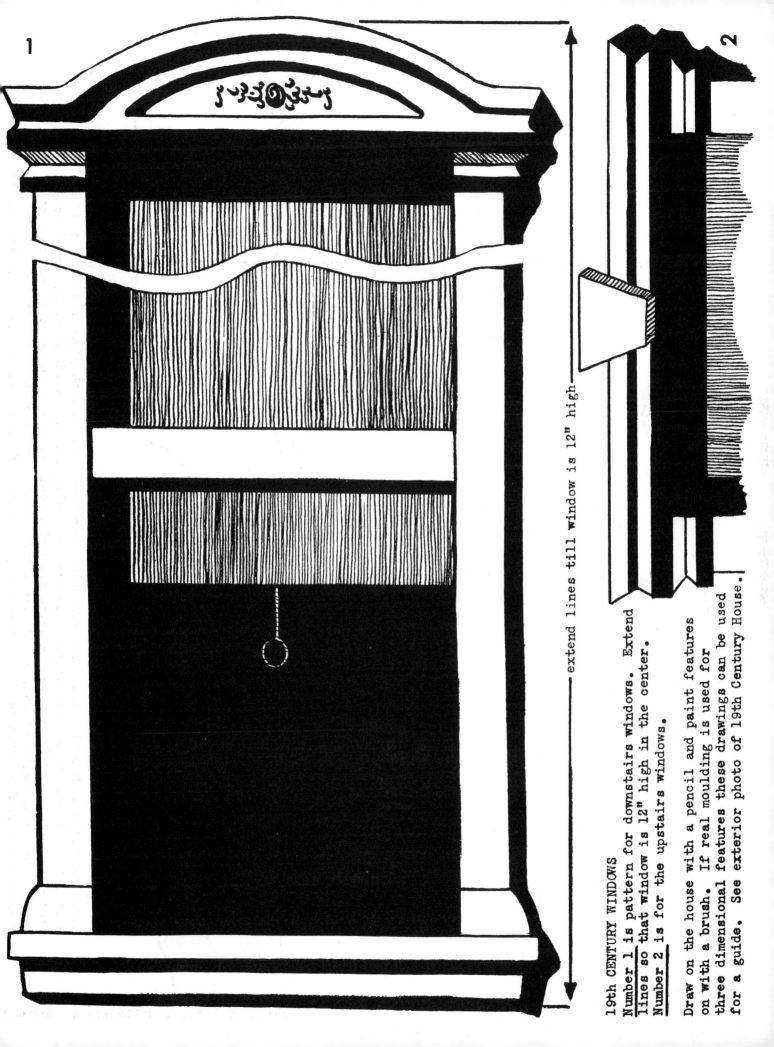

1

2

extend lines till window is 12" high

19th CENTURY WINDOWS

Number 1 is pattern for downstairs windows. Extend
lines so that window is 12" high in the center.
Number 2 is for the upstairs windows.

Draw on the house with a pencil and paint features
on with a brush. If real moulding is used for
three dimensional features these drawings can be used
for a guide. See exterior photo of 19th Century House.

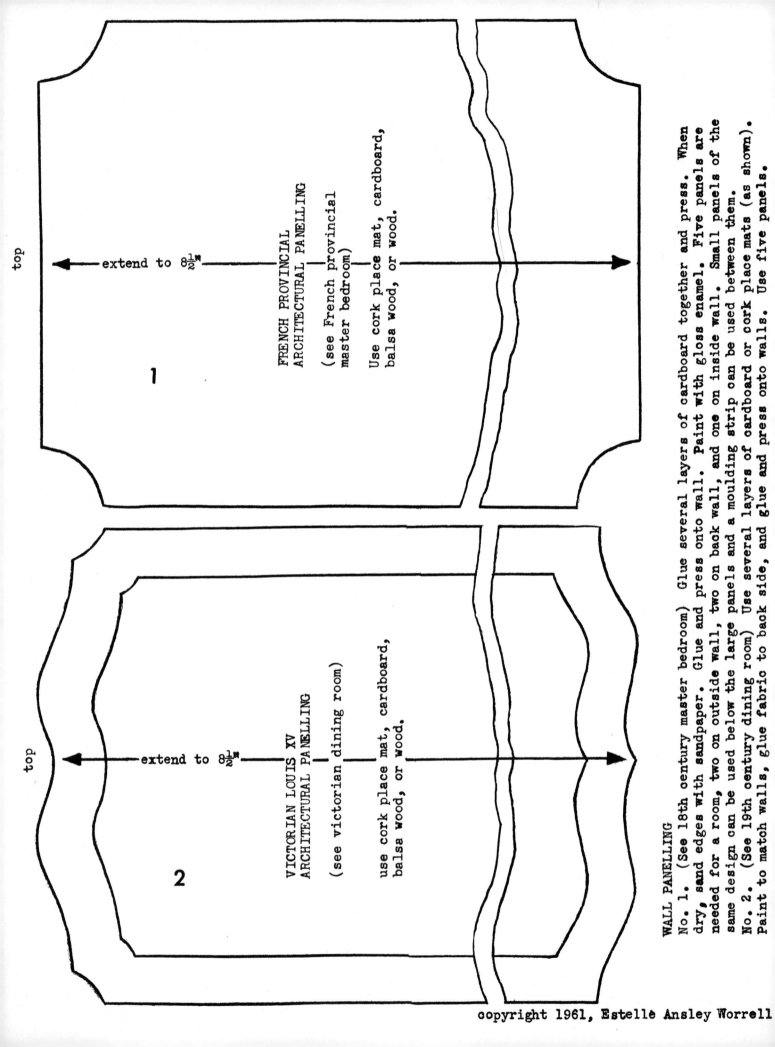

top

← extend to $8\frac{1}{2}$" →

FRENCH PROVINCIAL
ARCHITECTURAL PANELLING

(see French provincial
master bedroom)

Use cork place mat, cardboard,
balsa wood, or wood.

1

top

← extend to $8\frac{1}{2}$" →

VICTORIAN LOUIS XV
ARCHITECTURAL PANELLING

(see victorian dining room)

use cork place mat, cardboard,
balsa wood, or wood.

2

WALL PANELLING

No. 1. (See 18th century master bedroom) Glue several layers of cardboard together and press. When dry, sand edges with sandpaper. Glue and press onto wall. Paint with gloss enamel. Five panels are needed for a room, two on outside wall, two on back wall, and one on inside wall. Small panels of the same design can be used below the large panels and a moulding strip can be used between them. No. 2. (See 19th century dining room) Use several layers of cardboard or cork place mats (as shown). Paint to match walls, glue fabric to back side, and glue and press onto walls. Use five panels.

18th CENTURY MANTEL

1. Cut mantel 8" high X 7½" wide with a 4" X 4" opening centered. Use 1" thick wood or styrofoam. (Some boxes are suitable)
2. If styrofoam is used it should be covered with cloth, balsa wood, cardboard, vinyl, etc.
3. Cut mantel shelf 1¼" wide X 8" long, from balsa wood or cardboard.
4. Cut pediment from wood, cardboard, or balsa wood. Cut hearth from same. (6" X 2")
5. Glue mantel, shelf, pediment, and hearth onto a piece of black paper. The paper will hold the entire mantel together so that it can easily be glued into house. The black also gives depth to the fireplace by showing in the opening. Press till dry.
6. Glue balsa wood strips for moulding as indicated. Actual pressed wood mouldings can be used for a professional touch, if desired. Trim away paper.
7. Sand edges with sandpaper. Dust.
8. Paint with white gloss enamel. Because of the variety of materials used it will probably be necessary to apply two coats. Leave inside fireplace opening black.
9. A mirror or picture can be glued into the pediment.
10. Pressed wood decorations, lace or plastic doily cut-outs can be glued on for carving.

Andirons are lamp finials. Candle holders are chrome drawer pulls. Fire screen is cloth covered cardboard, an applicator stick, a pill bottle cap and a ___ bead.

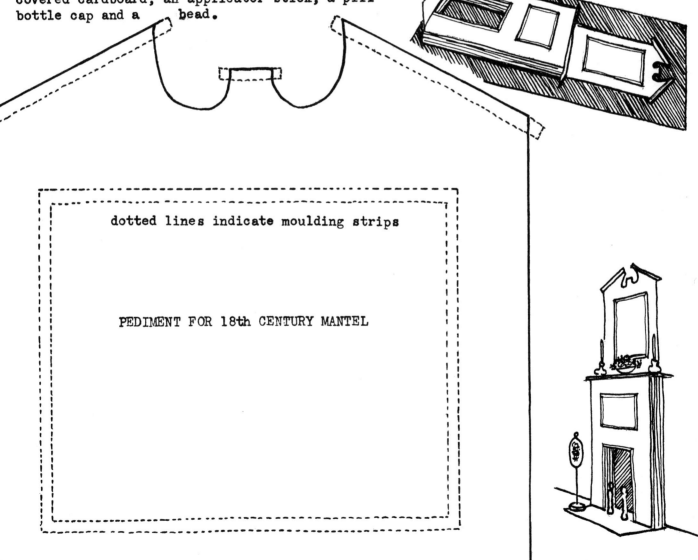

dotted lines indicate moulding strips

PEDIMENT FOR 18th CENTURY MANTEL

This pattern can also be used for a bed headboard   [65]

Number 1 (See 17th century living room) This one was made of 1" thick styrofoam covered with "stones" cut from a cork place mat. (Cardboard, sandpaper, or rough cloth can be used). Cut 7½" high and about 8" wide, with a 4" X 4" fireplace opening. Use vinyl, cardboard, balsa wood, plywood, etc., for hearth and shelf. Paint or cover inside of fireplace a dark color for depth.

Number 2 was made of wood. (See 17th century kitchen). Coathanger wire was used for crane which really moves. Put two cup hooks in the side, bend wire into shape, place into hooks, pinch hooks closed with pliers, and it not only moves but it will not come out. See diagram. If styrofoam is used for this style, cover with sandpaper, and glue in hairpins to hold crane. See no. 1 for shelf and hearth. An oven opening can be cut in it, if desired.
Use parts of plastic doilies, painted black, for trivets and lids to icing containers in canned cinnamon rolls for "pewter" plates. Individual jelly containers can be used for plates also.

Number 3 was also made of wood. (Styrofoam can be covered with cloth, cardboard, or balsa wood.) (See 19th century parlor and nursery.) Make about 8" X 8" with a 4" X 4" fireplace opening. Round the top of the opening. Add lace, jewelry, plastic doily cut-outs, pressed wood decorations, etc., for carving. See no. 1 for hearth and shelf. Paint with white gloss enamel. While paint is still wet, dip a thread in black, brown, or gray paint and wiggle it across it for a "marble" surface. Use glass drawer pulls for crystal candle holders, lamp finials for andirons.

Number 4 should have the same dimensions as no. 3. Use pencils, coathanger tubes, half paper towel rolls, etc., for columns for a classic style. Use balsa wood strips, applicator sticks or cardboard for moulding. See no 3 for marble finish. Use bottle caps for vases. Frame a purse mirror with gold braid.

Number 5 should be smaller than the other mantels for an authentic French Victorian style. Make it 6½" X 6½". Make the fireplace opening about 3" X 3", with a rounded top. The dark area on the drawing was usually iron on the real mantels. Grates for coal were used. Various plastic baskets can be cut down for a miniature grate. Decorate mantel with lace, braid, jewelry, etc., for carving. See no. 3 for marble finish.

For authentic 18th century mantel and pediment see pattern.

A variety of materials such as boxes, wood, styrofoam, cardboard, ceramic tiles, wood or plastic toy bricks, etc. can be used for all these mantels.

The styrofoam can be covered with cloth, cork, sandpaper, adhesive paper, vinyl, ceramic tile, balsa wood, cardboard, etc.. Some cloth actually has a stone or brick pattern! Plain cloth can be quilted in the shape of stones or bricks for a realistic effect!

Do not glue mantel to wall until you have tried several room arrangements with the furniture to be used with it.

Many gift stores have fine brass candle holders, wood baskets, warming pans, china vases, pill boxes, and other miniatures which are perfect in size and elegant in looks. Shop owners rarely consider them toys, however, so you may have to browse around to discover them for yourself.

Several coats of paint may be necessary on mantels which use a variety of materials, in order to make all materials look the same.

17th CENTURY DESIGNS

The earliest designs in America were probably Dutch and German,
and were either brought here by the settlers or were done here from
memory. They were usually painted on chests, cabinets, chairs, tables,
wall panels, etc,. Sometimes they were done with nail heads. (This
can be done on the doll furniture with sequin pins.) Many of the
designs were religious or magical in nature and were called "hex signs."

Use these designs for a light pencil guide. Use a small brush and
paint right over the pencil lines. Use bright colors with black.
Use enamel or water paints or inks. It may be necessary to wipe the
surface with a damp cloth if paint rolls off. When the design is
completed and dry, shellac over it. (Plastic spray fixitive can be
used instead.) This not only protects the designs but it antiques
the furniture at the same time.

The designs can be used for needlework also. Embroider them on footstools, wall hangings, pillows, upholstery, firescreens, linens,
curtains, doll clothes, etc..

They can be used as guides for carving when plywood is used for the
furniture. Use them wherever designs are indicated.

[67]

BEDS, 17th CENTURY

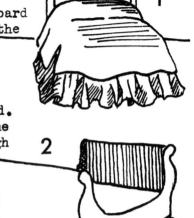

Number 1 was made with a laminated cardboard headboard. The banister-back chair pattern was used. Any of the other chair patterns can be used for a headboard also. The bed frame was made from 1" thick styrofoam covered with cloth. Beads were used for feet. The headboard was painted with brown gloss enamel. Make beds about 6" X 12" for the adult dolls, smaller for the 8" dolls.

Number 2 is a sleigh bed made from a cigar box and cardboard. The box top was cut in half and the two pieces glued to the box. The curved sides were cut to fit. They were made of laminated cardboard. (Five layers of laundry cardboard.) Beads were added for feet. The bed was sanded with sandpaper and painted with brown enamel. The sleigh bed is actually 19th century, but it goes well with any style.

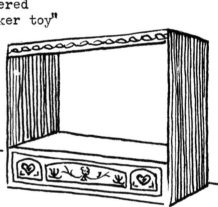

Number 3 was made of four clothespins and a sturdy box. This is a simple style recommended for beginners. Bead feet can be added to this old style low-post bed, if desired. The whole bed was painted with brown gloss enamel. The box can be covered with cloth and the clothespins shellacked for a different look.

Number 4, a Dutch cupboard bed, was made from a shoe box and cardboard. The box was cut down so that it is about 3" deep. It was used up-side-down and several layers of cardboard were glued together for the end pieces. The ends were glued to the box and its top. This can be covered with cloth or painted with enamel. See "17th Century Designs" for painted designs.

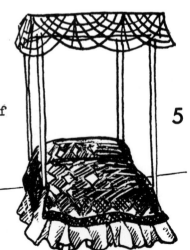

Number 5, shown in the 17th century nursery was made from a box, new pencils, and styrofoam. The fishnet canopy cover was made from a rectangular plastic doily. The styrofoam canopy was covered completely with muslin before being glued to the pencils. ("Tinker toy" sticks can be used for posts.) A quilt can be made with 1½" squares. This allows for ¼" seams. One block from a real quilt can be used if a border is added. There are also fabrics with a patchwork design print.

All these beds can be made with plywood, laminated cardboard, styrofoam, or sturdy boxes.

See needlework pages for bed cover patterns. Be sure to monogram the linens for future generations! Use batiste for the sheets and pillowcases and muslin for the mattresses. Knitted and crocheted bedspreads were common during the early years in America. They are the oldest of the needlecrafts. There are no directions given for them here, however, because so many patterns are available in needlework books which are authentic and well suited for miniatures. One square from afghan, bedspread, tablecloth, place mat, or doily patterns can be used and an edge of crochet, lace or fringe added to it to enlarge it.

The bed shown in the 17th century master bedroom is given on another page because it requires a special pattern.

Interestingly, there is a real antique bed which is called a pencil-post bed! It was an economical version of the elegant four poster bed with canopy. The posts were not spooled or carved, but were straight. The canopy was also straight!

FIELD BED (master bedroom)

1. Cut ten canopy side pieces from cardboard. (Use tablet back or laundry cardboard). Glue with white glue and press into two stacks of five pieces each as indicated. ($\frac{1}{2}$" styrofoam or wood can be used.)
2. Cut five braces from $\frac{1}{2}$" thick styrofoam and cover each with cloth. (Make each brace 1" X 5" if styrofoam or wood is used for the sides.) If cardboard is used it will not be as thick so the braces will need to be 1" X $5\frac{1}{2}$" to allow for the difference.
3. Assemble with pins and glue as indicated.
4. Make bed frame 12" long by 6" wide. Use 1" thick styrofoam and cover it completely with glue and cloth.
5. Punch small holes for posts with scissors point in corners of bed frame. Use four new pencils or other dowels for posts. Glue pencils into bed frame.
6. Insert pencil into each slot without glue to test fit before using glue. Glue canopy frame onto pencils. Pins may be needed to help hold pieces together while glue dries.
7. Use large beads or push-pins for feet. Beads can be added on top of canopy for finials also.
8. Paint with brown gloss enamel. White can be used for an 18th century French provincial bed.

Make canopy cover to fit. Make buttonholes for finials so it can be removed for washing. Cover shown was made of batiste and eyelet ruffles. A wider eyelet ruffle was used for the dust ruffle.

Use muslin or other cloth for mattress, and batiste or broadcloth for sheets. See needlework pages for bed covers.

Plywood can be used for this bed, and then stained for a natural finish. A headboard can be added, if desired. One of the chair, mantel or secretary pediments, or bureau patterns can be used for it.

Posts can be made with two clothespins. Each post will require two. This will give a spooled or turned look to the posts. Slight alterations will be necessary in pattern for this type.

cut ten

FIELD BED FRAME SIDE CANOPY

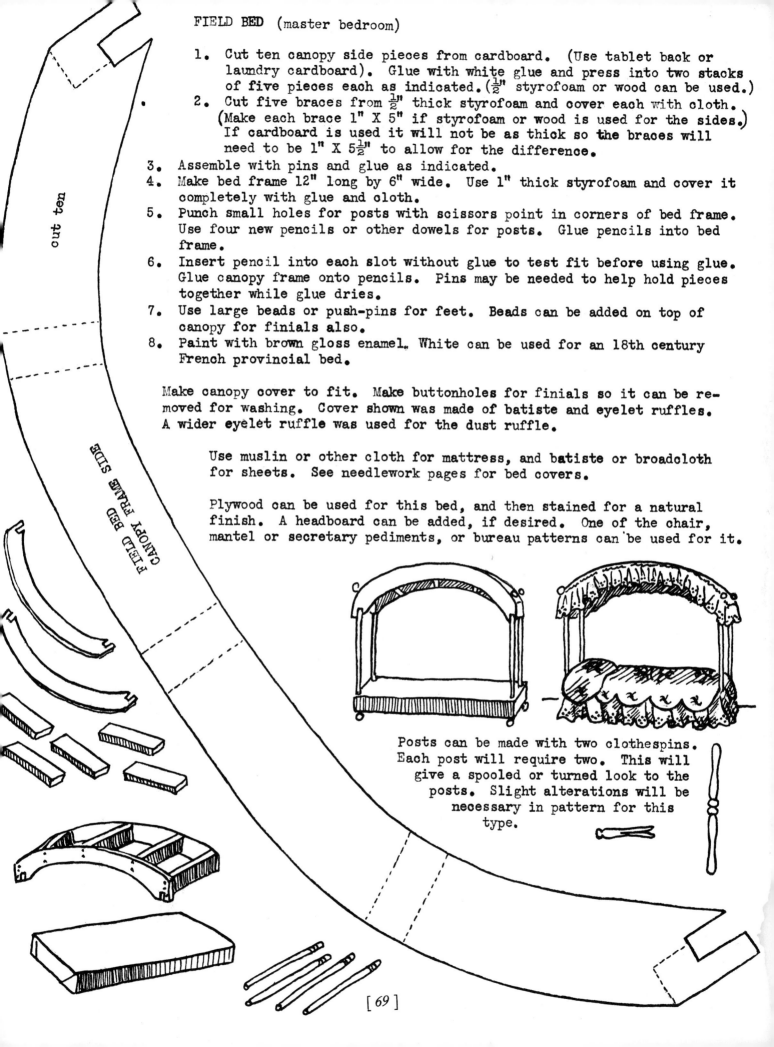

BANISTER-BACK CHAIR BACK

cut five

BANISTER-BACK CHAIR FRONT

cut five

BANISTER BACK CHAIR (master bedroom)

1. Cut five chair back pieces and five chair front pieces from cardboard, (laundry or tablet-back cardboard.)
2. Glue or laminate the layers together and press till dry. Spread white glue on with a brush.
3. Cut seat 2 3/4" wide X 2 1/4" deep. Use $\frac{1}{2}$" thick styrofoam. (If cardboard is used for seat, glue and press about ten layers together.) Side pieces should be 2 3/4" X 3/4".
4. Sand all edges with coarse sandpaper, then with fine sandpaper to smooth. Dust off.
5. Assemble as directed. Use sequin pins and glue. A rubber band or twine tied around chair will help hold securely till dry.
6. Glue a matchstem across the bottom of the banisters. This piece was left out to make cutting easier.
7. Glue matchstems, balsa wood strips, popsicle sticks, etc. for stretchers.
8. Paint with brown gloss enamel. For a smooth finish, sand with fine sandpaper and paint a second time.
9. For directions for rush seat see pattern for LADDER-BACK ROCKER.

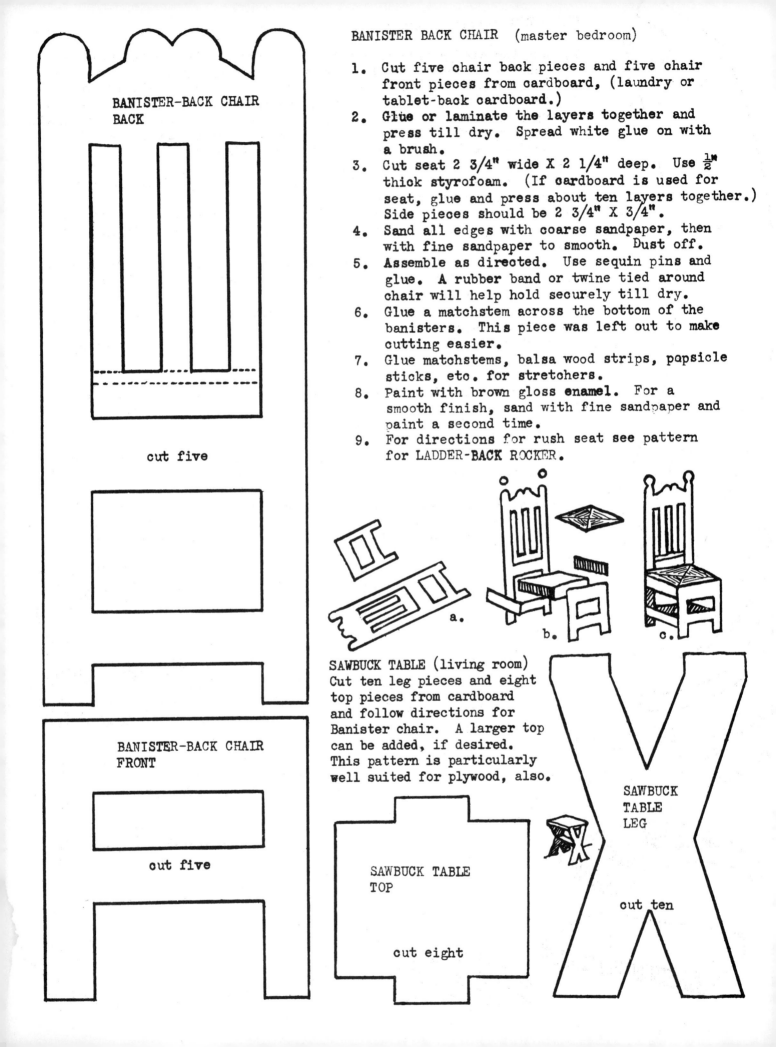

a.

b.

c.

SAWBUCK TABLE (living room)
Cut ten leg pieces and eight top pieces from cardboard and follow directions for Banister chair. A larger top can be added, if desired. This pattern is particularly well suited for plywood, also.

SAWBUCK TABLE TOP

cut eight

SAWBUCK TABLE LEG

cut ten

WING BACK CHAIR OR EMPIRE CHAIR (nursery, 18th C. dining room)
1. Use quart milk carton (or cardboard). Place pattern
   around carton and draw around it. Cut on lines.
2. Cover outside back of chair with white glue and place
   onto cloth (about 12" X 8"), which has been spread out
   flat. Outside of cloth should face down.
3. Cover sides of chair with glue and finish placing cloth.
4. Trim fabric to about ½" around edges of chair and
   clip as indicated. Fold edges over and glue.
5. Use chair pattern for inside upholstery piece.
   Glue into place. Bend out wings slightly while
   still damp, for a sculptured look.
6. Stuff newspaper into bottom of chair for
   weight and to help hold seat in place while
   glue dries. Pad and cover seat. Make
   seat 2 5/8" X 2 5/8" from ½" styrofoam.

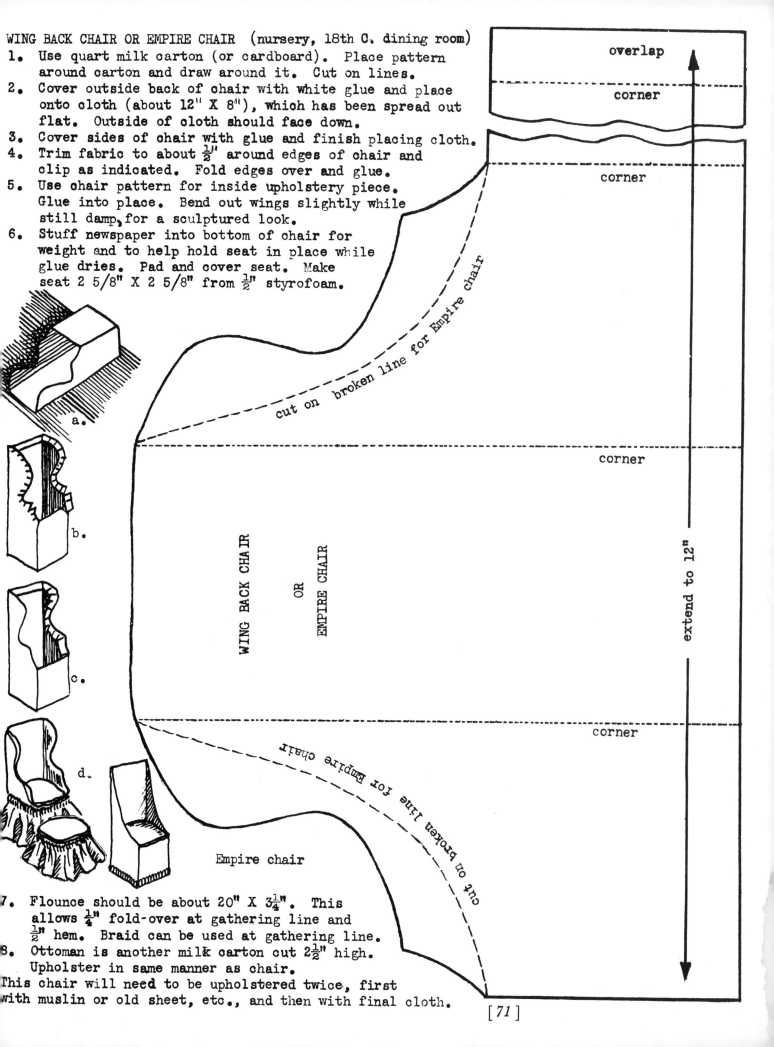

overlap

corner

corner

corner

corner

extend to 12"

cut on broken line for Empire chair

cut on broken line for Empire chair

WING BACK CHAIR

OR

EMPIRE CHAIR

a.

b.

c.

d.

Empire chair

7. Flounce should be about 20" X 3¼". This
   allows ¼" fold-over at gathering line and
   ½" hem. Braid can be used at gathering line.
8. Ottoman is another milk carton cut 2½" high.
   Upholster in same manner as chair.
This chair will need to be upholstered twice, first
with muslin or old sheet, etc., and then with final cloth.

[71]

WING BACK COUCH (living room)

1. Use "Giant" or "King" size soap or detergent box.
2. Place pattern around box as indicated and draw around it.
3. Cut with razor blade or kitchen knife.
4. Upholstery should be done twice for strength. Use muslin or old sheet for the first upholstery.
5. Cover outside back of couch with white glue and place, back side down, onto cloth about 27" X $7\frac{1}{4}$" which has been spread out flat. Be sure outside of fabric is down.
6. Cover ends with glue and fold cloth around. Glue front.
7. Trim fabric to about 3/4" around edges of couch and clip as indicated. Fold edges over and glue as indicated.
8. Use couch pattern for inside upholstery piece. Glue into place. Bend out or "sculpture" the wings and back slightly while still damp.
9. Cut seat 3 5/8" X 8 7/8". Use 1" thick styrofoam or several layers of cardboard. Stuff newspapers into the bottom to add weight and to help hold seat in place while glue dries. Pad and cover seat, glue into place.
10. Flounce should be 3" wide and $1\frac{1}{2}$ yards long. This allows for $\frac{1}{2}$" hem at the bottom and $\frac{1}{4}$" hem at gathering line. Gather and glue onto couch.

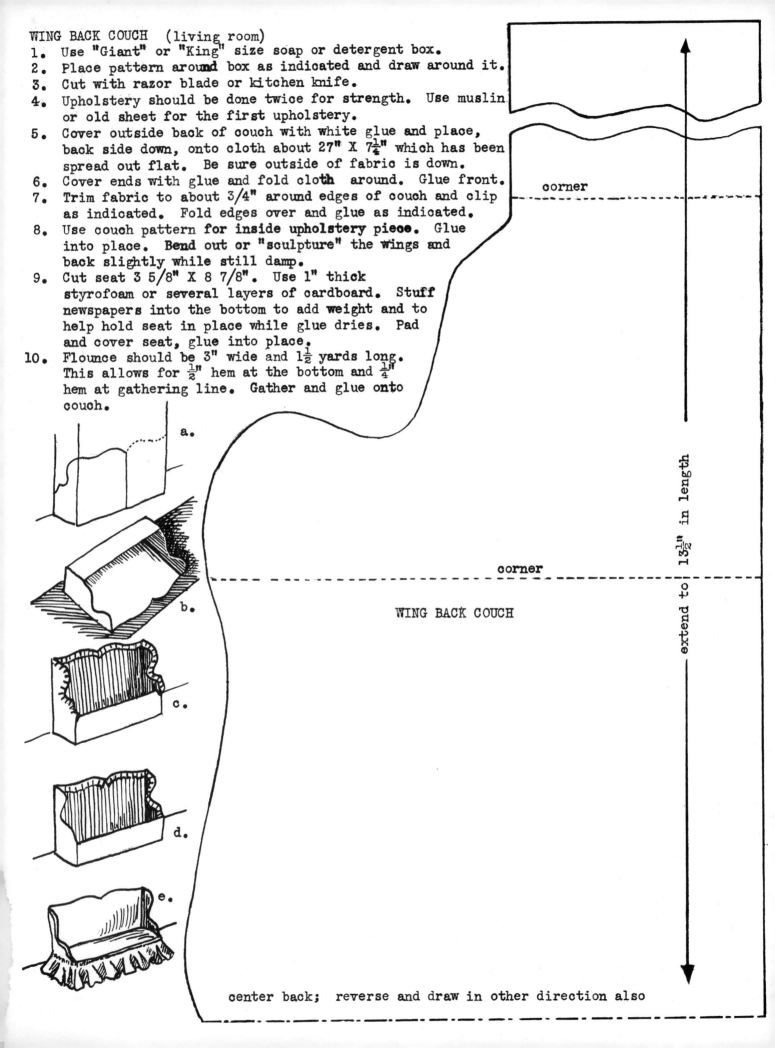

corner

corner

extend to $13\frac{1}{2}$" in length

WING BACK COUCH

a.

b.

c.

d.

e.

center back; reverse and draw in other direction also

VARIATIONS, 17th CENTURY PATTERNS

1. WAINSCOT CHAIR Use chair on p. 70 and leave back solid. Add panels of cardboard as shown.
2. WAINSCOT CHAIR WITH CANING Cut out back and seat of chair pattern on p. 70. Glue needlepoint canvas or net between layers of cardboard during construction.
3. CHARLES II CHAIR Same as no. 1, use lace for carving and add arms.
4. SPLAT-BACK CHAIR Leave center part of chair back solid and cut out two side openings of chair on p. 70. Add lace for carving. Use front legs from p. 101.
5. FIDDLE-BACK CHAIR is similiar to no. 4 with top rounded and center splat cut as shown.
6. CHARLES II SETTEE is no. 4 repeated with arms added.
7. CRADLE-CHAIR Repeat chair pattern of p. 76 and add cradle side.
8. HUTCH TABLE Use chair on p. 76 with back cut down to arm level. Attach table top with a cloth hinge.
9. CHAISE LOUNGE Use cereal or soap box sideways. Cut legs as shown. (p. 71)
10. WING CHAIR Use half gallon milk carton for pattern on p. 72. Cut legs as shown. Add cardboard seat.
11. WING CHAIR Same as no. 10 but slide pattern down so you use bottom of carton as shown. Use leg from p. 97 for front, popcicle stick for back.
12. QUEEN ANNE SOFA Use pattern of p. 72 in same manner as no. 11. Center leg pattern is from p. 75.
13. SETTLE Make back of couch on p. 72 higher and straight. Add cardboard layers to strengthen. Make seat of seven layers of cardboard and attach with cloth hinge so it will open. Add cardboard panels as shown.
14. WING BACK SOFA Use pattern on p. 72 and cut as shown. The legs are stronger if you round the corners of the cut-out as shown. Add seat of seven layers of cardboard.

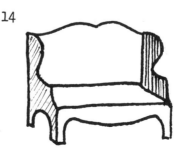

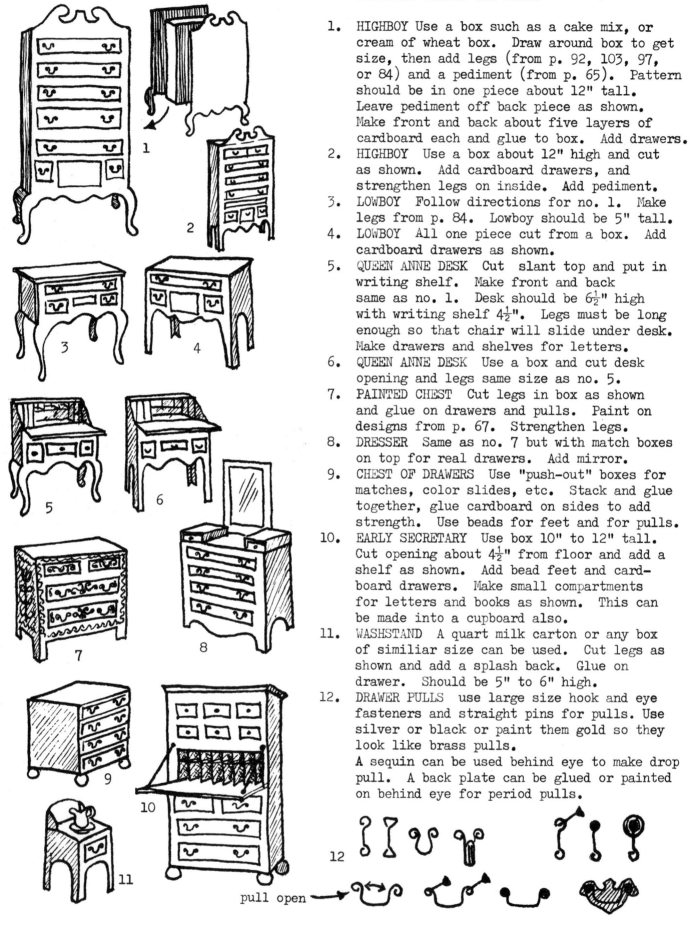

1. HIGHBOY Use a box such as a cake mix, or cream of wheat box. Draw around box to get size, then add legs (from p. 92, 103, 97, or 84) and a pediment (from p. 65). Pattern should be in one piece about 12" tall. Leave pediment off back piece as shown. Make front and back about five layers of cardboard each and glue to box. Add drawers.
2. HIGHBOY Use a box about 12" high and cut as shown. Add cardboard drawers, and strengthen legs on inside. Add pediment.
3. LOWBOY Follow directions for no. 1. Make legs from p. 84. Lowboy should be 5" tall.
4. LOWBOY All one piece cut from a box. Add cardboard drawers as shown.
5. QUEEN ANNE DESK Cut slant top and put in writing shelf. Make front and back same as no. 1. Desk should be $6\frac{1}{2}$" high with writing shelf $4\frac{1}{2}$". Legs must be long enough so that chair will slide under desk. Make drawers and shelves for letters.
6. QUEEN ANNE DESK Use a box and cut desk opening and legs same size as no. 5.
7. PAINTED CHEST Cut legs in box as shown and glue on drawers and pulls. Paint on designs from p. 67. Strengthen legs.
8. DRESSER Same as no. 7 but with match boxes on top for real drawers. Add mirror.
9. CHEST OF DRAWERS Use "push-out" boxes for matches, color slides, etc. Stack and glue together, glue cardboard on sides to add strength. Use beads for feet and for pulls.
10. EARLY SECRETARY Use box 10" to 12" tall. Cut opening about $4\frac{1}{2}$" from floor and add a shelf as shown. Add bead feet and cardboard drawers. Make small compartments for letters and books as shown. This can be made into a cupboard also.
11. WASHSTAND A quart milk carton or any box of similiar size can be used. Cut legs as shown and add a splash back. Glue on drawer. Should be 5" to 6" high.
12. DRAWER PULLS use large size hook and eye fasteners and straight pins for pulls. Use silver or black or paint them gold so they look like brass pulls.
A sequin can be used behind eye to make drop pull. A back plate can be glued or painted on behind eye for period pulls.

pull open ⟶

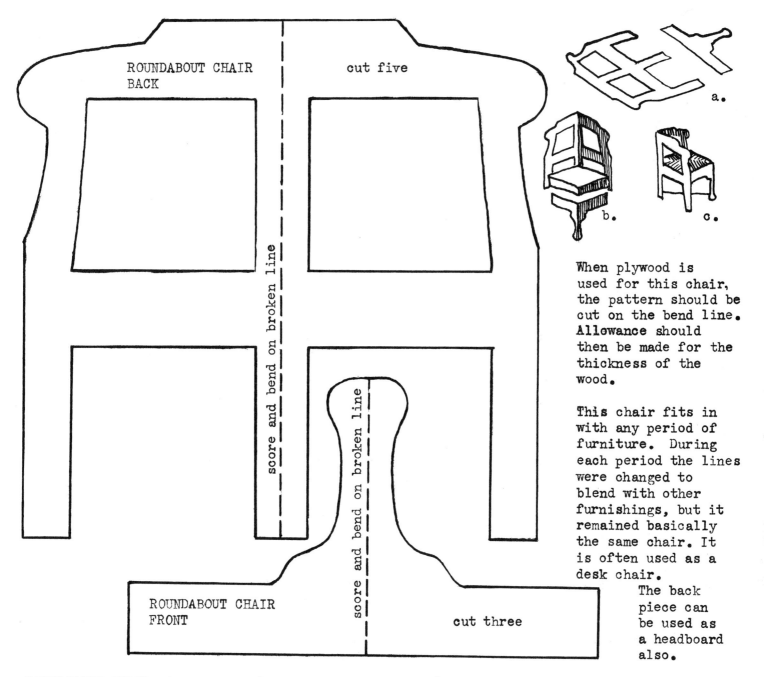

ROUNDABOUT CHAIR
BACK   cut five

score and bend on broken line

score and bend on broken line

ROUNDABOUT CHAIR
FRONT   cut three

a.

b.

c.

When plywood is used for this chair, the pattern should be cut on the bend line. Allowance should then be made for the thickness of the wood.

This chair fits in with any period of furniture. During each period the lines were changed to blend with other furnishings, but it remained basically the same chair. It is often used as a desk chair.

The back piece can be used as a headboard also.

ROUNDABOUT CHAIR (living room)

1. Cut five chair back pieces. Cut three chair front pieces. (Use laundry or tablet-back cardboard.)
2. Score on broken lines by pulling scissors point along a ruler and making an impression in the cardboard. This will make the bend neat and straight.
3. Glue five back pieces together with white glue and press around a corner of a milk carton, box, etc.. Tie with twine to hold tight till glue dries. Repeat with the three front pieces. (A pencil or other dowel can be used for the front leg instead of the cardboard piece, if preferred.)
4. Cut seat $2\frac{1}{2}$" X $2\frac{1}{2}$". Use $\frac{1}{2}$" thick styrofoam. (If cardboard is used for the seat, use about ten layers, glue and press.)
5. Sand all edges with coarse sandpaper. Repeat with fine sandpaper to smooth edges.
6. Assemble with sequin pins and glue. Tie a string around chair, at seat line, to hold till glue dries. Glue a matchstem in the crease on the inside of the front leg to add strength.
7. Use applicator sticks, balsa wood strips, or popsicle sticks for stretchers.
8. Paint with brown gloss enamel. Sand again with fine paper and paint a second time.
9. For seat, pad and cover a piece of cardboard the same size as the seat, or make a rush seat. See LADDER-BACK ROCKER.

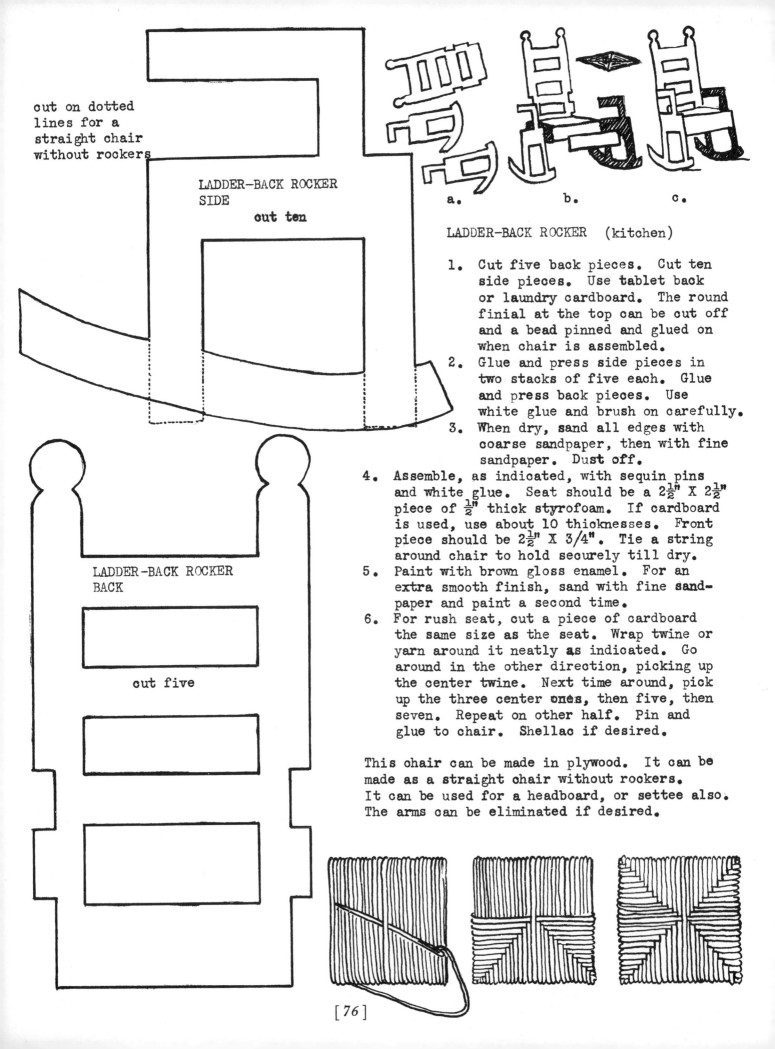

cut on dotted
lines for a
straight chair
without rockers

LADDER-BACK ROCKER
SIDE

cut ten

a.   b.   c.

LADDER-BACK ROCKER
BACK

cut five

LADDER-BACK ROCKER (kitchen)

1. Cut five back pieces. Cut ten
   side pieces. Use tablet back
   or laundry cardboard. The round
   finial at the top can be cut off
   and a bead pinned and glued on
   when chair is assembled.
2. Glue and press side pieces in
   two stacks of five each. Glue
   and press back pieces. Use
   white glue and brush on carefully.
3. When dry, sand all edges with
   coarse sandpaper, then with fine
   sandpaper. Dust off.
4. Assemble, as indicated, with sequin pins
   and white glue. Seat should be a $2\frac{1}{2}"$ X $2\frac{1}{2}"$
   piece of $\frac{1}{2}"$ thick styrofoam. If cardboard
   is used, use about 10 thicknesses. Front
   piece should be $2\frac{1}{2}"$ X 3/4". Tie a string
   around chair to hold securely till dry.
5. Paint with brown gloss enamel. For an
   extra smooth finish, sand with fine sandpaper and paint a second time.
6. For rush seat, cut a piece of cardboard
   the same size as the seat. Wrap twine or
   yarn around it neatly as indicated. Go
   around in the other direction, picking up
   the center twine. Next time around, pick
   up the three center ones, then five, then
   seven. Repeat on other half. Pin and
   glue to chair. Shellac if desired.

This chair can be made in plywood. It can be
made as a straight chair without rockers.
It can be used for a headboard, or settee also.
The arms can be eliminated if desired.

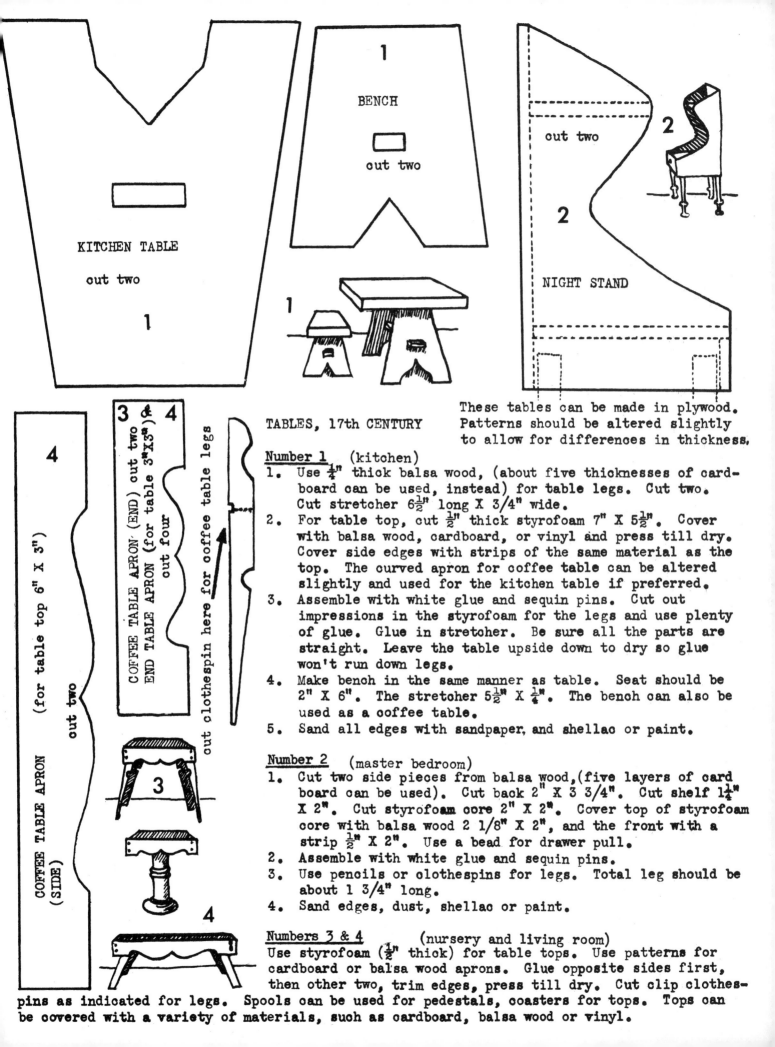

KITCHEN TABLE

out two

1

1

BENCH

out two

1

cut two

2

NIGHT STAND

2

4

(for table top 6" X 3")

out two

COFFEE TABLE APRON (SIDE)

3 & 4

COFFEE TABLE APRON (END) out two

END TABLE APRON (for table 3"X3")
out four

cut clothespin here for coffee table legs

3

4

These tables can be made in plywood.
Patterns should be altered slightly
to allow for differences in thickness.

TABLES, 17th CENTURY

Number 1   (kitchen)
1. Use ¼" thick balsa wood, (about five thicknesses of cardboard can be used, instead) for table legs. Cut two.
   Cut stretcher 6½" long X 3/4" wide.
2. For table top, cut ½" thick styrofoam 7" X 5½". Cover
   with balsa wood, cardboard, or vinyl and press till dry.
   Cover side edges with strips of the same material as the
   top. The curved apron for coffee table can be altered
   slightly and used for the kitchen table if preferred.
3. Assemble with white glue and sequin pins. Cut out
   impressions in the styrofoam for the legs and use plenty
   of glue. Glue in stretcher. Be sure all the parts are
   straight. Leave the table upside down to dry so glue
   won't run down legs.
4. Make bench in the same manner as table. Seat should be
   2" X 6". The stretcher 5½" X ¼". The bench can also be
   used as a coffee table.
5. Sand all edges with sandpaper, and shellac or paint.

Number 2   (master bedroom)
1. Cut two side pieces from balsa wood,(five layers of card
   board can be used). Cut back 2" X 3 3/4". Cut shelf 1¼"
   X 2". Cut styrofoam core 2" X 2". Cover top of styrofoam
   core with balsa wood 2 1/8" X 2", and the front with a
   strip ½" X 2". Use a bead for drawer pull.
2. Assemble with white glue and sequin pins.
3. Use pencils or clothespins for legs. Total leg should be
   about 1 3/4" long.
4. Sand edges, dust, shellac or paint.

Numbers 3 & 4   (nursery and living room)
Use styrofoam (½" thick) for table tops. Use patterns for
cardboard or balsa wood aprons. Glue opposite sides first,
then other two, trim edges, press till dry. Cut clip clothes-
pins as indicated for legs. Spools can be used for pedestals, coasters for tops. Tops can
be covered with a variety of materials, such as cardboard, balsa wood or vinyl.

CROMWELLIAN CHAIR (kitchen)

1. Cut seat 2 3/4" X 2 3/4" from 1" thick styrofoam.
2. Cut back 2 3/4" X 2 3/4" from ½" thick styrofoam.
3. Assemble as indicated with white glue and matchstems or toothpicks.
4. Upholster with heavy brown cloth to resemble the old leather upholstery or a printed cloth to resemble the old "turkey-work" cloth.
5. Cut clip type clothespin legs as indicated and glue into place after punching holes for them with scissors point. (Pencils, 3" hairpins, other type clothespins, popsicle sticks, etc., can be used. See no. 4)
6. The back can be shortened and used with posts as in no. 2.
7. The back can be cut with various curved designs as in no. 3.

This is probably the easiest chair of all, and is a good one for beginners.

When laminated cardboard is used, use about ten layers for the seat and about five for the back. The back can be cut in any shape and it can be curved slightly by bending it around a jar while still damp.

It can be made with plywood also.

HIGH CHAIR (kitchen)

1. Cut five back pieces and ten side pieces from cardboard (laundry or tablet back type). The top finials can be cut off and beads glued on later, if preferred.
2. Glue and press the five back pieces together. Glue the side pieces together in two stacks of five each.
3. Cut seat 2" X 2". Use ½" thick styrofoam. (If cardboard is used glue about ten layers together.) Cut front piece 2" X 3/4".
4. Sand all edges with sandpaper. Dust.
5. Assemble with sequin pins and glue, as indicated. Tie a string around chair to hold pieces in place till dry. Use matchstems, balsa wood, or popsicle sticks for stretchers.
6. Paint with brown enamel. Sand with fine sandpaper, dust, and paint again.
7. Seat can be balsa wood, cardboard covered with cloth, or a rush seat of twine. (See LADDER BACK ROCKER for directions.)

HIGH CHAIR BACK

cut five

HIGH CHAIR SIDE cut ten

a.

b.

No. 2

No. 3

a.

b.

No. 4

[78]

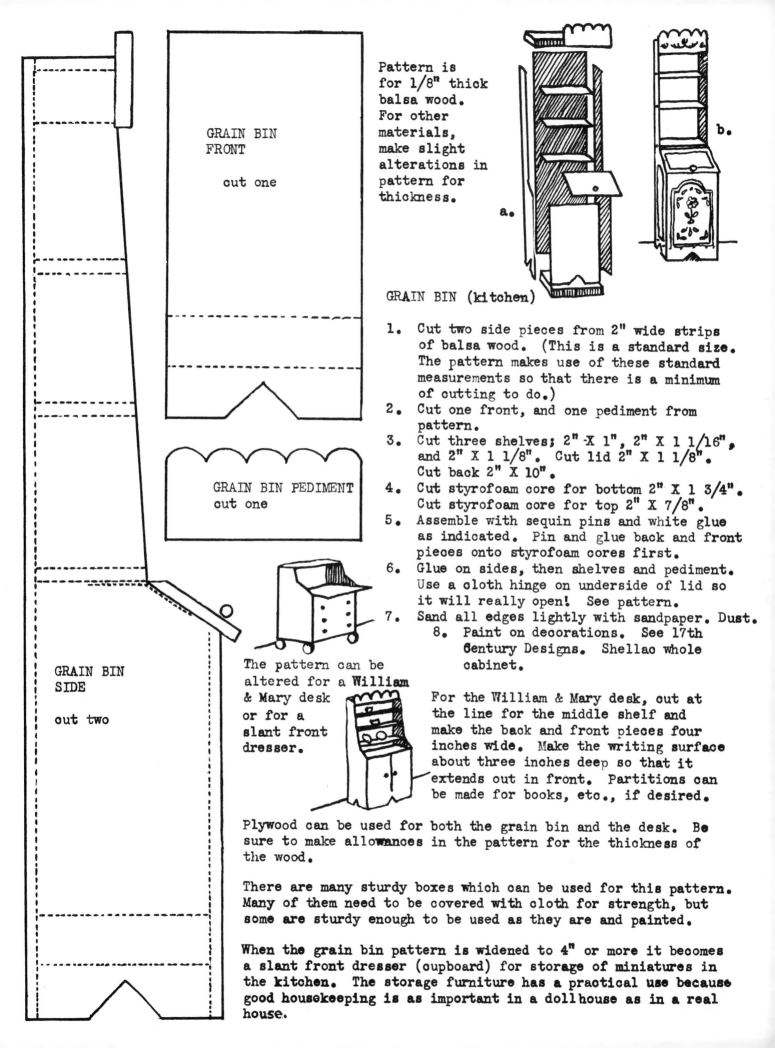

GRAIN BIN
FRONT

cut one

Pattern is
for 1/8" thick
balsa wood.
For other
materials,
make slight
alterations in
pattern for
thickness.

GRAIN BIN PEDIMENT
cut one

GRAIN BIN
SIDE

cut two

GRAIN BIN (kitchen)

1. Cut two side pieces from 2" wide strips of balsa wood. (This is a standard size. The pattern makes use of these standard measurements so that there is a minimum of cutting to do.)
2. Cut one front, and one pediment from pattern.
3. Cut three shelves; 2" X 1", 2" X 1 1/16", and 2" X 1 1/8". Cut lid 2" X 1 1/8". Cut back 2" X 10".
4. Cut styrofoam core for bottom 2" X 1 3/4". Cut styrofoam core for top 2" X 7/8".
5. Assemble with sequin pins and white glue as indicated. Pin and glue back and front pieces onto styrofoam cores first.
6. Glue on sides, then shelves and pediment. Use a cloth hinge on underside of lid so it will really open! See pattern.
7. Sand all edges lightly with sandpaper. Dust.
8. Paint on decorations. See 17th 6entury Designs. Shellac whole cabinet.

The pattern can be altered for a **William & Mary desk** or for a **slant front dresser.**

For the William & Mary desk, cut at the line for the middle shelf and make the back and front pieces four inches wide. Make the writing surface about three inches deep so that it extends out in front. Partitions can be made for books, etc., if desired.

Plywood can be used for both the grain bin and the desk. Be sure to make allowances in the pattern for the thickness of the wood.

There are many sturdy boxes which can be used for this pattern. Many of them need to be covered with cloth for strength, but some are sturdy enough to be used as they are and painted.

When the grain bin pattern is widened to 4" or more it becomes a slant front dresser (cupboard) for storage of miniatures in the kitchen. The storage furniture has a practical use because good housekeeping is as important in a dollhouse as in a real house.

18th CENTURY DESIGNS

Most 18th century designs were French inspired, either directly from France or by way of the English designers who also were looking to France.

The shell, the arabesque, and the column were popular. They were dainty and feminine and formally balanced. Later in the century they became heavier and more masculine as designers turned to classic forms.

Some of these designs can be used for stencils but they are actually intended for guides. Make a light pencil drawing on the furniture, and then paint on gold paint with a small brush. They will fit most tables, chests, chairs, cabinets, beds, wall panels, etc.. The designs can be shellacked over when dry for an antique finish but with most gold paints it isn't necessary in order to protect the paint.

The 19th century designs can be used on 18th century furniture because many of them were copied during the Victorian era.

They can also be used as patterns for needlework on such items as firescreens, foot stools, pillows, wall hangings, linens, doll clothes, upholstery, curtains, etc.. Use any type embroidery stitch, particularly outline and satin stitch.

They can be used for guides for carving on all types of plywood doll furniture where designs are indicated.

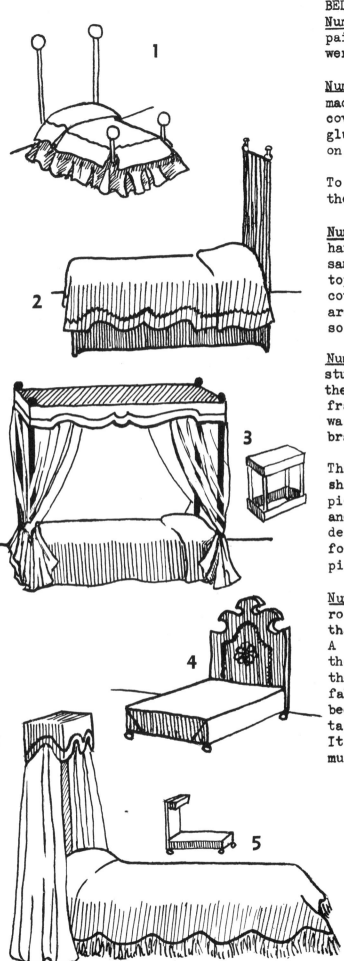

BEDS, 18th CENTURY

<u>Number 1</u> was made from a candy box with gold painted pencils for posts. Small styrofoam balls were covered with glitter and attached to posts.

<u>Number 2</u>, shown in the 18th century nursery, was made from a cigar box. The box and its top were covered seperately with cotton percale and then glued together. Pushpins were used for decoration on the headboard.

To cover, paint evenly with glue and then put on the fabric as though "wrapping a present."

<u>Number 3</u> was made from a box. Paper tubes from pants hangers were used for posts. Posts should all be the same length. Glue them on the inside of the box and its top with plenty of glue. Glue beads on top. The canopy cover and bed spread match and the attached curtains are sheer nylon. Buttonholes were made for the beads so the cover can be removed for laundering.

<u>Number 4</u> was made of styrofoam. (A box can be stuffed with folded newspapers and glued together for the bed with cardboard for the headboard.) The bed frame is 1" thick and the headboard $\frac{1}{2}$" thick. It was upholstered in corduroy and trimmed with gold braid and old jewelry. Beads were used for feet.

The bed frame should be 12" X 6". The headboard should be 10" X 6". For the curved shape, cut a piece of paper 10" X 6", fold in half lengthwise and cut a design across the top. When a pleasing design is found, use it for a pattern on the styrofoam. It will be easier to upholster the two pieces separately and then join with pins and glue.

<u>Number 5</u>, shown in the 18th century master bedroom, was made in the same manner as no. 4 except that the top of the headboard was left straight. A 6" X 2" piece of 1" thick styrofoam covered with the same fabric as the bed should be glued onto the headboard for the little canopy. A cotton fabric was used for the canopy cover and matching bed spread. Sheer fabric was used for the curtains which are attached to the canopy cover. It all comes off for laundering. The mattress is muslin, the linens are batiste and lace.

The methods of constructing the beds and the materials used in them can both be interchanged for many variations.

They can all be made of plywood and stained for an authentic and permanent piece of furniture.

[81]

LOUIS XV SIDE CHAIR (master bedroom)

1. Wrap pattern around scouring powder
   can amd draw.
2. Cut with razor blade or kitchen
   knife.
3. Cut eight leg sections from
   cardboard (laundry or tablet
   back type).
4. Score leg sections on dotted lines
   by running scissors point along line.
5. Glue on leg sections. It will be
   necessary to use a rubber band or
   cord around chair to hold legs in
   place while glue dries. Paper clips
   or clothespins should be used
   to hold legs together.
6. Repeat, using the other four leg
   sections over those already
   glued on.
7. Glue a toothpick or match
   stem in the joint on the
   underside of the chair legs
   to give extra strength.
8. When glue is dry, sand edges
   with coarse sandpaper and
   then smooth with fine
   sandpaper. Be sure to
   wipe off dust.
9. Glue on lace rosettes or
   braid for carving.
10. Paint with gloss enamel.
    For an extra smooth finish,
    sand with very fine sand-
    paper and then paint again.
    Carving can be gilded with
    gold paint if desired.
11. Pad and cover back and seat
    cushions and glue in. Seat should
    be 2 5/8" in diameter. Use styrofoam or cardboard. Back cushion is
    drawn in dotted line on chair pattern. Use cardboard for back cushion.
12. For a simpler version, use the extra tall can and make the seat 2 3/4"
    from the bottom. Flounce should be 20" X 3 1/2" allowing 1/2" hem
    at bottom and 1/4" at gathering line .

This chair can be made in cardboard. Use several layers glued
and pressed together.

It can be upholstered completely, if preferred.

Legs, such as clothespins (both types), pencils, etc. can be used.

LOUIS XV SIDE CHAIR
LEG SECTION
cut eight

score and bend

score and bend

LOUIS XV SIDE CHAIR

dotted line is pattern for back cushion

style no. 1   style no. 2

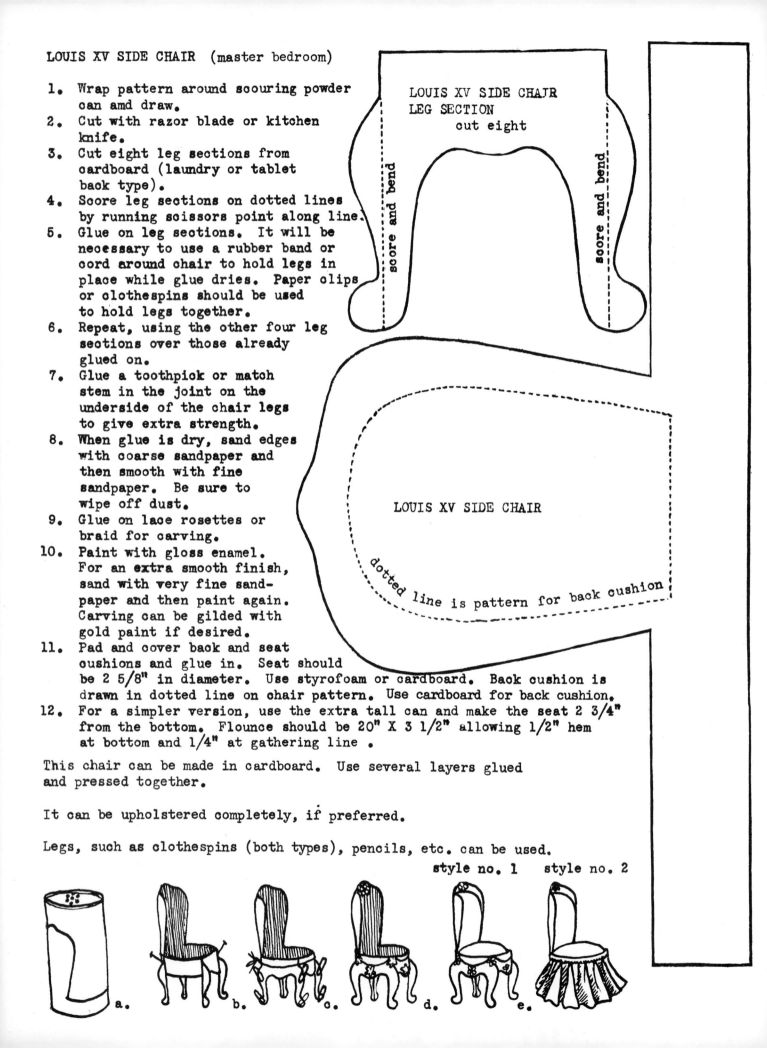

a.   b.   c.   d.   e.

1. QUEEN ANNE CHAIR Use back of chair on p. 92 with chair on p. 94.
2. LOUIS XVI CHAIR Make an oval back on chair on p. 94 with or without arms. This same shape can be an ADAM or HEPPLEWHITE chair.
3. HEPPLEWHITE SHIELD BACK CHAIR Use chair of page 94 with a shield-shaped back. Use small pins for nail head designs.
4. LOUIS XV CHAIR Use pattern on p. 92 with back left solid or partly cut out.
5. ROCOCO CHAIR Use pattern on p. 92 with the back squared and the front leg pattern repeated on the back.
6. LOUIS XV END CHAIR This chair, on p.94 can have the legs bent in many ways. This style shows them bent out, in, then out again at the feet. Press with your fingers and shape at the same time while glue is still damp. Seat can be a $2\frac{7}{8}$" rounded square, pear shape or circle. Mold chair to fit.
7. CHIPPENDALE CHAIR Use pattern on p. 92 and square the corners as shown.
8. COLONIAL SLAT-BACK CHAIR Trace back of chair pattern on p.85 onto pattern of page 92.
9. PEASANT CHAIR Use back of pattern on p. 88 on upper back part of chair on p. 101.
10. DESK OR VANITY CHAIR Use chair on p.94 and make a low rounded back as shown, about 2" high.
11. LOUIS XV SOFA Pattern on p. 94 was extended $4\frac{1}{2}$" for sofa. Extend seat $4\frac{1}{2}$" to make oblong and use seven layers of cardboard.
12. CHIPPENDALE SETTEE Repeat pattern on p. 92 as shown. Make seat $\frac{1}{2}$" deeper. Back can be left solid.
13. WING CHAIR Trace pattern for chair on p. 90 with leg from p. 97. Trace straight edge of upper front of leg on straight line of front of chair. For wing see p. 72. Round back of chair as shown.
14. DUNCAN PHYFE SOFA Combine pattern on p. 90 with one on p. 91 so sofa ends and legs are in one piece. Cut out sides and curve arm as shown.
15. SHERATON SOFA Use couch pattern p. 91. Place up about $1\frac{1}{2}$" from bottom of box. Cut legs as shown. Make seat seven layers of cardboard.

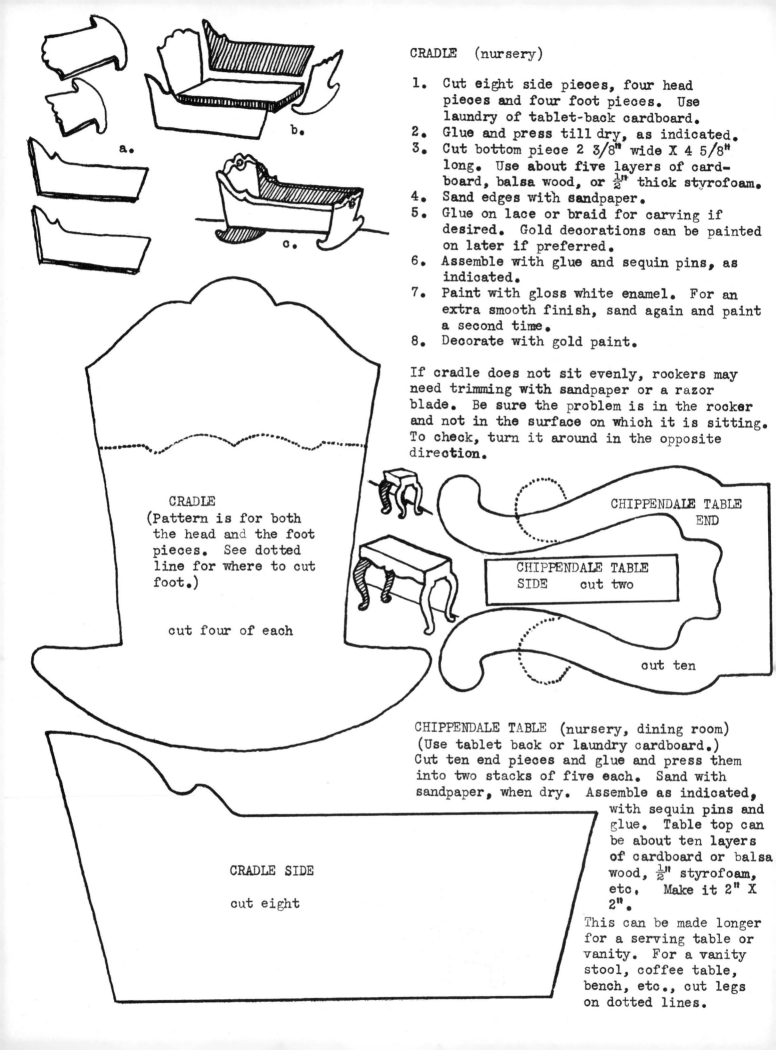

CRADLE (nursery)

1. Cut eight side pieces, four head pieces and four foot pieces. Use laundry of tablet-back cardboard.
2. Glue and press till dry, as indicated.
3. Cut bottom piece 2 3/8" wide X 4 5/8" long. Use about five layers of cardboard, balsa wood, or $\frac{1}{2}$" thick styrofoam.
4. Sand edges with sandpaper.
5. Glue on lace or braid for carving if desired. Gold decorations can be painted on later if preferred.
6. Assemble with glue and sequin pins, as indicated.
7. Paint with gloss white enamel. For an extra smooth finish, sand again and paint a second time.
8. Decorate with gold paint.

If cradle does not sit evenly, rockers may need trimming with sandpaper or a razor blade. Be sure the problem is in the rocker and not in the surface on which it is sitting. To check, turn it around in the opposite direction.

CRADLE
(Pattern is for both the head and the foot pieces. See dotted line for where to cut foot.)

cut four of each

CHIPPENDALE TABLE END

CHIPPENDALE TABLE SIDE   cut two

cut ten

CHIPPENDALE TABLE (nursery, dining room)
(Use tablet back or laundry cardboard.)
Cut ten end pieces and glue and press them into two stacks of five each. Sand with sandpaper, when dry. Assemble as indicated, with sequin pins and glue. Table top can be about ten layers of cardboard or balsa wood, $\frac{1}{2}$" styrofoam, etc. Make it 2" X 2".

This can be made longer for a serving table or vanity. For a vanity stool, coffee table, bench, etc., cut legs on dotted lines.

CRADLE SIDE

cut eight

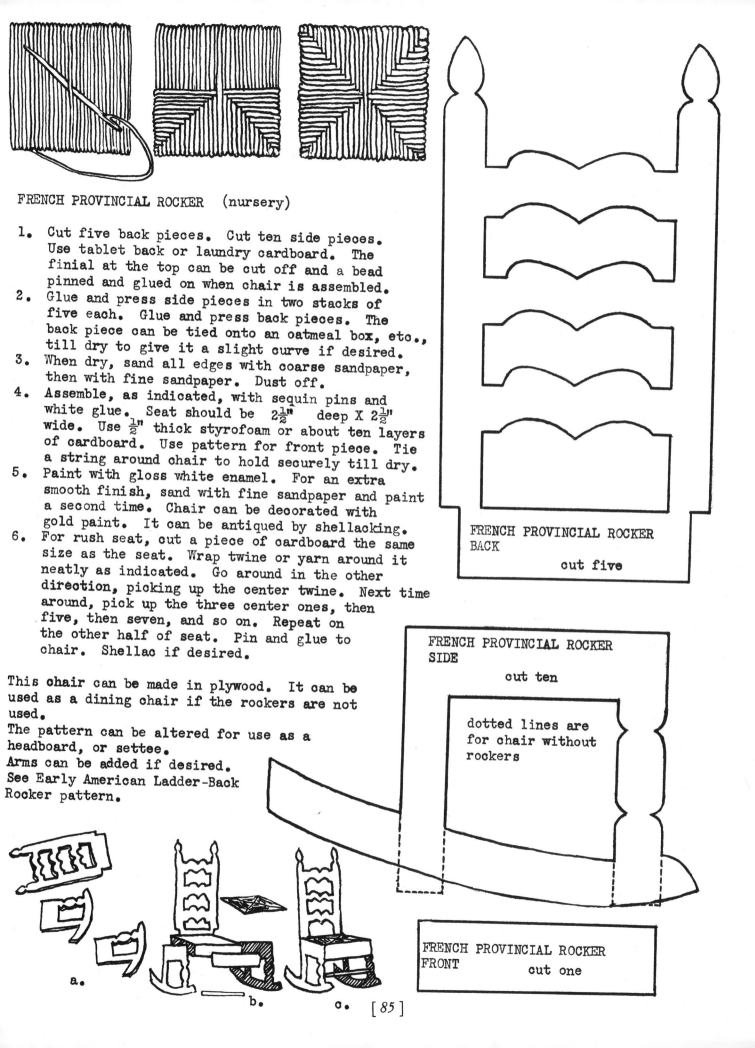

FRENCH PROVINCIAL ROCKER (nursery)

1. Cut five back pieces. Cut ten side pieces. Use tablet back or laundry cardboard. The finial at the top can be cut off and a bead pinned and glued on when chair is assembled.
2. Glue and press side pieces in two stacks of five each. Glue and press back pieces. The back piece can be tied onto an oatmeal box, etc., till dry to give it a slight curve if desired.
3. When dry, sand all edges with coarse sandpaper, then with fine sandpaper. Dust off.
4. Assemble, as indicated, with sequin pins and white glue. Seat should be $2\frac{1}{2}$" deep X $2\frac{1}{2}$" wide. Use $\frac{1}{2}$" thick styrofoam or about ten layers of cardboard. Use pattern for front piece. Tie a string around chair to hold securely till dry.
5. Paint with gloss white enamel. For an extra smooth finish, sand with fine sandpaper and paint a second time. Chair can be decorated with gold paint. It can be antiqued by shellacking.
6. For rush seat, cut a piece of cardboard the same size as the seat. Wrap twine or yarn around it neatly as indicated. Go around in the other direction, picking up the center twine. Next time around, pick up the three center ones, then five, then seven, and so on. Repeat on the other half of seat. Pin and glue to chair. Shellac if desired.

This chair can be made in plywood. It can be used as a dining chair if the rockers are not used.
The pattern can be altered for use as a headboard, or settee.
Arms can be added if desired.
See Early American Ladder-Back Rocker pattern.

FRENCH PROVINCIAL ROCKER
BACK

cut five

FRENCH PROVINCIAL ROCKER
SIDE

cut ten

dotted lines are for chair without rockers

FRENCH PROVINCIAL ROCKER
FRONT   cut one

a.

b.

c.

No. 1 can also be used for a plant or candle stand. Make top 2" in diameter.

END TABLE PEDESTAL 1 cut five

cut five 1 END TABLE PEDESTAL

These tables can easily be made in plywood. Be sure that allowances are made for the thickness of the wood.

overlap

corner

make table top $7\frac{1}{2}$" X $5\frac{1}{2}$"

1

make table top 3" in diameter   cut one

APRON FOR ROUND END TABLE

2   cut seven

DINING TABLE PEDESTAL

corner

make table top $7\frac{1}{2}$" X $5\frac{1}{2}$"

make table top $7\frac{1}{2}$" X $5\frac{1}{2}$"   cut two

cut seven

2

DINING TABLE PEDESTAL

END APRON FOR DINING TABLE   cut two

SIDE APRON FOR DINING TABLE

2

corner

overlap

overlap

2

corner

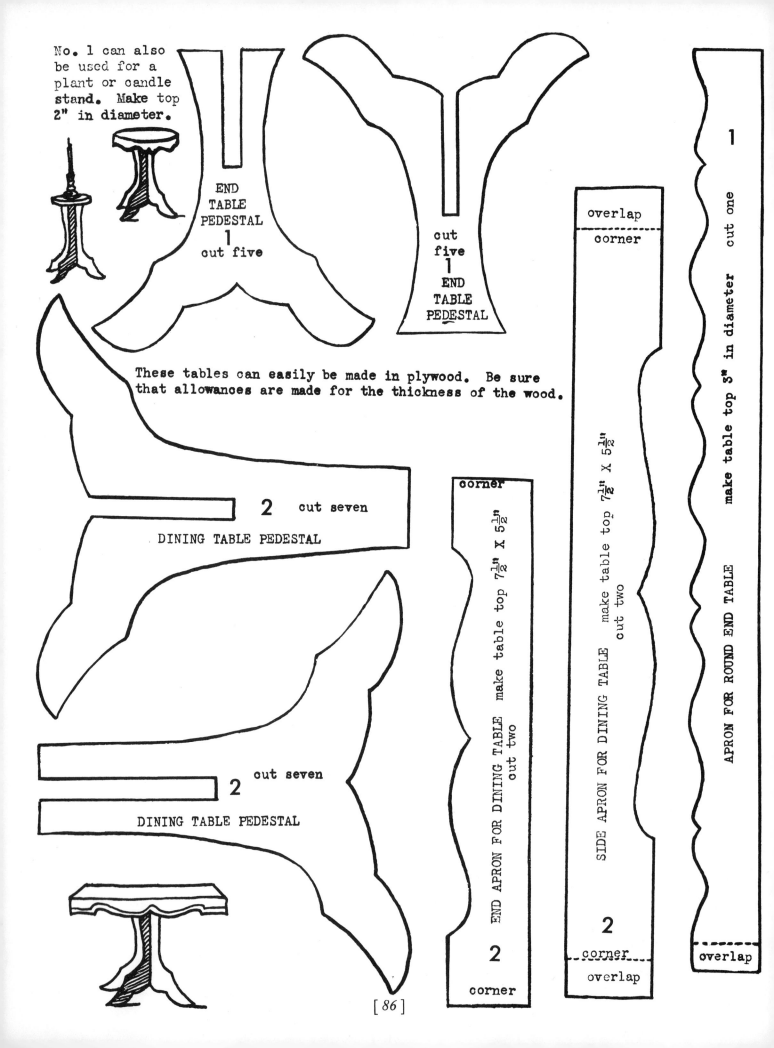

1 and 2

1. Cut five of each pedestal piece for no. 1. Cut seven layers of cardboard for each pedestal piece for no. 2. Glue and press.
2. Trim and sand with sandpaper.
3. Join two sections as shown on p. 86. Slot them together dry, first, to see if they fit, then glue them.
4. Glue seven to ten layers of cardboard together for table tops. Press till dry. Box tops make good table tops. Round face powder boxes make round table tops.

3

1. Measure the box top to be used for the table top and make leg pattern fit. Leg section should fit up inside the top. Cut eight of each leg section. Glue and press. See figures a. and b. below.
2. The top can be strengthened with extra cardboard inside if necessary. Stretchers can be used if needed.

4

Use leg patterns from p. 70, 82, 84, 92, 101, or 103 for benches, coffee tables, stools, lamp tables, and so on. They can be used flat or crossed and slotted as shown.

5

Use front leg section from p. 75 for tables cut from quart milk cartons and other boxes. Pattern fits on corner of carton at bottom.

6

Tables of all sizes and shapes can be cut from boxes. Strengthen legs on the inside with dowels, sticks, cardboard, etc.

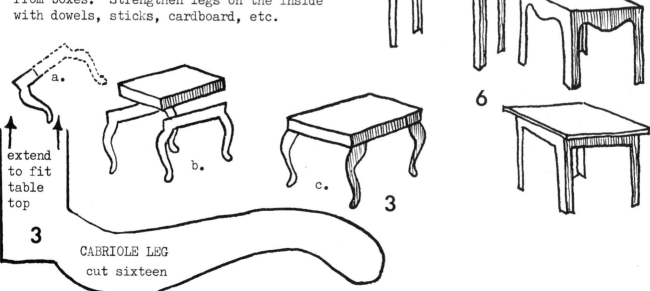

extend
to fit
table
top

CABRIOLE LEG
cut sixteen

guide for painted decoration around chair seat

corner

corner

PEASANT CHAIR
SIDE

corner

corner

PEASANT CHAIR
BACK

cut five

guide for painted
decorations

This can be used as a stencil
or for a guide for a light
pencil outline for brush
painting. If water color, etc,
is used wipe surface with a
damp cloth first.

PEASANT CHAIR (nursery)

1. Cut five chair back pieces. (Use tablet backs or laundry
   cardboard.)
2. Glue or laminate the layers together and press till dry.
3. Cut seat $2\frac{1}{2}"$ X $2\frac{1}{2}"$ from $\frac{1}{2}"$ styrofoam. Cut cardboard piece
   the same size and glue and press the two together.
4. Glue side piece around seat.
5. Glue back onto seat as indicated. Tie with a string to
   hold pieces in position till dry. Pins can be used to help
   hold side piece in place. When painted they look like nails.
6. Put clothespin legs into place as indicated. Slant back legs
   slightly.
7. Sand all edges with coarse sandpaper, then smooth the edges
   with fine sandpaper.
8. Paint with gloss enamel.
9. Decorate. The designs can be painted on with gold paint.
   They can be painted on with colored enamel or with water
   color, ink, or tempera. If water color, ink, or tempera
   is used, chair should be shellacked when designs are dry.
10. If preferred, chair can be trimmed with a Scandinavian
    type braid trim, $\frac{1}{2}"$ wide.

This pattern can be
used for plywood.
It makes a suitable
kitchen chair for any
style house.

cut clip type
clothespin here

a.   b.   c.   d.

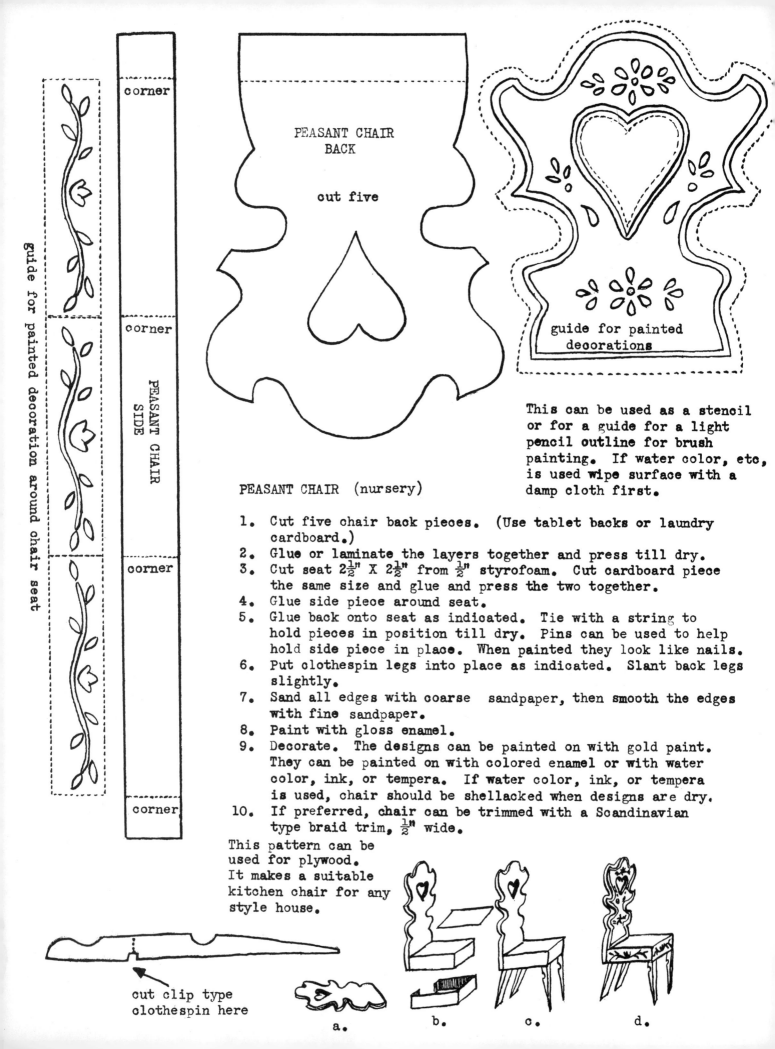

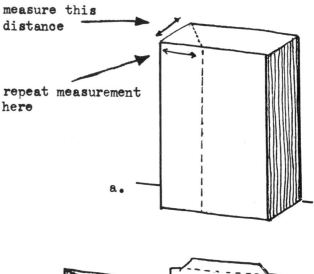

measure this distance

repeat measurement here

a.

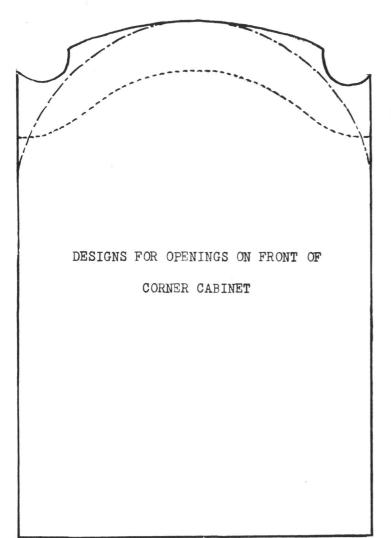

DESIGNS FOR OPENINGS ON FRONT OF

CORNER CABINET

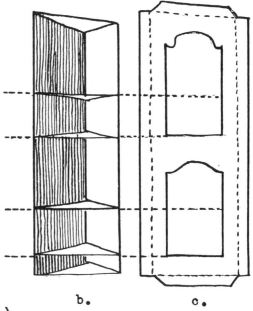

b.   c.

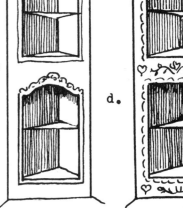

d.

CORNER CABINET   (dining room and 17th century living room)

1. Use large detergent or soap box.
2. Measure depth of box. Measure the same distance across the top and bottom of the box from the same corner so that the two sides of the triangle are the same.
3. Draw a line between the points and cut. Cut sides.
4. Use top for pattern for shelves. Use balsa wood or several thicknesses of cardboard. Use pins and glue.
5. Lay, open side down, on cardboard and draw around cabinet for the front piece. Add 1" around for overlapping. Cut corners as indicated. Score bend lines by pulling scissors point down line along a ruler. This impression will make a straight and neat bend. Cut front openings.
6. Glue front onto cabinet. Pin into place.
7. Sand edges lightly. Paint with gloss enamel.
8. Glue on lace, braid or plastic doily for carving for 18th century style.
9. For 17th century style, paint on designs. Use water color (wipe surface with damp cloth first), enamel, ink, or tempera. Shellac cabinet when designs are dry. This protects designs and gives an antique finish at same time.
10. For a special colorful effect, paint the inside of the cabinet with a bright color. This pattern can easily be adapted to plywood for any style furniture. It can be glued into the dollhouse permanently. Make triangles approximately 4" X 4" X 5 3/4". Make cabinet about 14" high.

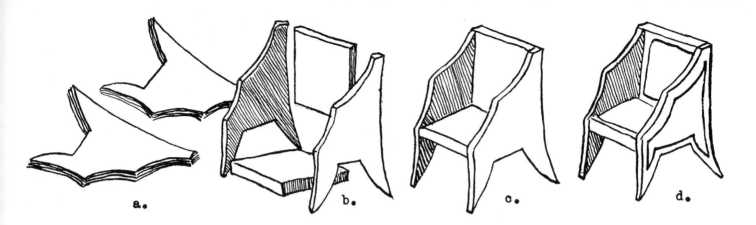

a. b. c. d.

LOUIS XVI CHAIR (dining room)

1. Cut sixteen chair side pieces from cardboard. (Use tablet backs or laundry cardboard.)
2. Glue eight pieces together. Glue other eight pieces together in the same manner and press till dry.
3. Glue eight (3 3/4" deep X 3 1/4" wide) seat pieces together and press.
4. Glue eight (3 1/2" high X 3 1/4" wide) back pieces together in the same manner and press till dry.
5. Assemble with pins and glue. Be sure not to confuse seat and back pieces during assembly.
6. When thoroughly dry, sand all edges with coarse sandpaper. Smooth edges with fine sandpaper.
7. Paint with gloss enamel. For an extra smooth finish, sand with fine sandpaper and then paint a second time.
8. Chair can be gilded in manner indicated on pattern, if desired.
9. Lace, braid or plastic doily cut-outs can be glued on for carving.
10. Seat and back cushions can be added.

Plywood can be used for this pattern. Because of its simplicity, it is suggested for beginners.

It can be made in either corrugated cardboard or styrofoam and then upholstered. Use clip clothespin legs. The Wing Back Chair upholstery pattern can be altered slightly to fit.

This type chair can be used in most any room in the house. Leave it plain for the dining room, or upholster it for the living room. Cushions can be used in either type.

The design can be put on with narrow gold braid trim instead of paint. Use pins to hold in place while glue dries.

Many other finishes and types of decoration can be used for this chair. It is a good piece on which to experiment!

cut sixteen

LOUIS XVI CHAIR
SIDE

dotted lines indicate where to put trim

This pattern can also be used for a couch. Make back and seat pieces about 8" wide.

[90]

center back; **reverse and draw in other direction**

LOUIS XVI COUCH

corner fold

extend pattern to 13½"

corner

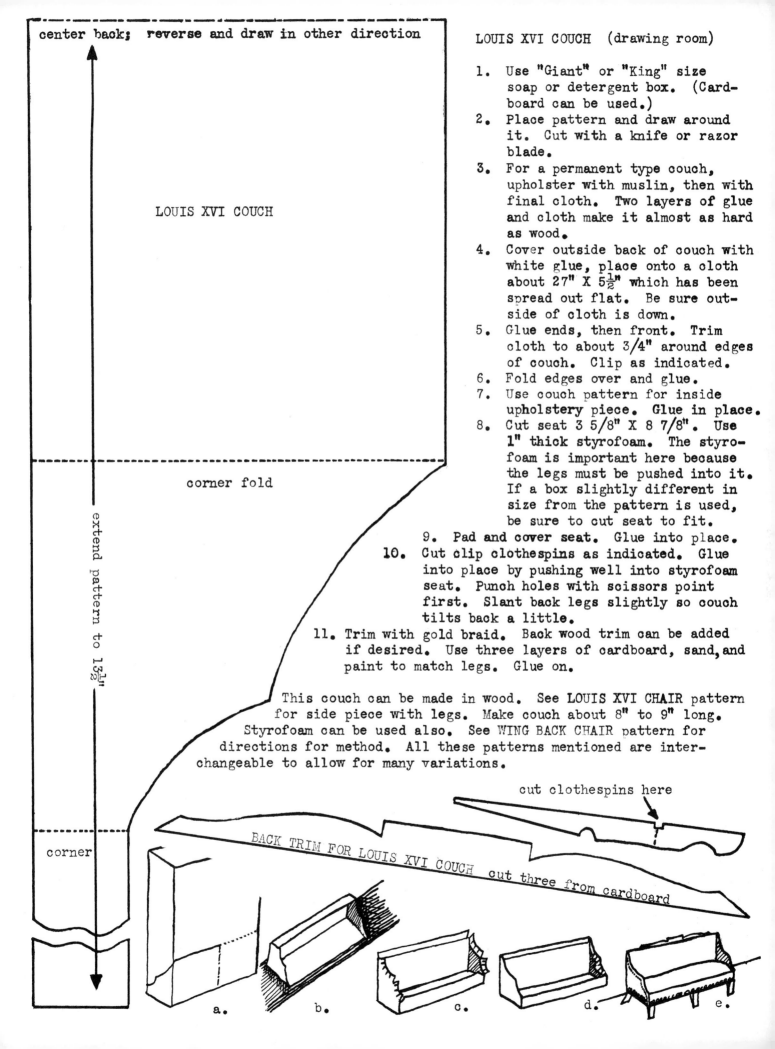

LOUIS XVI COUCH (drawing room)

1. Use "Giant" or "King" size soap or detergent box. (Cardboard can be used.)
2. Place pattern and draw around it. Cut with a knife or razor blade.
3. For a permanent type couch, upholster with muslin, then with final cloth. Two layers of glue and cloth make it almost as hard as wood.
4. Cover outside back of couch with white glue, place onto a cloth about 27" X 5½" which has been spread out flat. Be sure outside of cloth is down.
5. Glue ends, then front. Trim cloth to about 3/4" around edges of couch. Clip as indicated.
6. Fold edges over and glue.
7. Use couch pattern for inside upholstery piece. Glue in place.
8. Cut seat 3 5/8" X 8 7/8". Use 1" thick styrofoam. The styrofoam is important here because the legs must be pushed into it. If a box slightly different in size from the pattern is used, be sure to cut seat to fit.
9. Pad and cover seat. Glue into place.
10. Cut clip clothespins as indicated. Glue into place by pushing well into styrofoam seat. Punch holes with scissors point first. Slant back legs slightly so couch tilts back a little.
11. Trim with gold braid. Back wood trim can be added if desired. Use three layers of cardboard, sand, and paint to match legs. Glue on.

This couch can be made in wood. See LOUIS XVI CHAIR pattern for side piece with legs. Make couch about 8" to 9" long. Styrofoam can be used also. See WING BACK CHAIR pattern for directions for method. All these patterns mentioned are interchangeable to allow for many variations.

cut clothespins here

BACK TRIM FOR LOUIS XVI COUCH cut three from cardboard

a.   b.   c.   d.   e.

CHIPPENDALE CHAIR (drawing room)

1. Cut five chair back pieces from cardboard. (laundry or tablet back cardboard)
2. Cut five chair front pieces.
3. Glue or laminate the layers together and press till dry.
4. Cut seat 2 5/8" wide X 2 1/4" deep. Use $\frac{1}{2}$" thick styrofoam. (If cardboard is used, glue about ten layers together)
5. Sand back and front pieces with coarse sandpaper to even edges, and then fine sandpaper to smooth them. Dust off.
6. Glue all pieces together as indicated. Use pins to attach side pieces. A rubber band or twine around the chair will help hold it together till the glue dries.
7. Glue on plastic doily cut-outs or lace to look like carving.
8. Matchstems or balsa wood strips can be used for stretchers if needed.
9. Paint with gloss enamel. For an extra smooth finish, sand with very fine sandpaper and then paint a second time. Use off-white enamel as shown in the 18th century living room or use brown enamel to look like natural wood.
10. Cut cardboard the same size as the seat. Pad and then cover with fabric. Glue onto seat for cushion. Use pins or twine to hold tight and flat till glue dries.
11. The carving can be gilded if desired.

This style is particularly well suited for a dining room chair.

This pattern can be used for plywood. If plywood is used, it can actually be carved and stained for an authentic effect.

The design is based on one of Chippendale's early pieces. During his early career he was influenced by the Queen Anne styles, therefore if it is used without the carving and in a natural finish, it becomes a Queen Anne Chair.

The front legs can be used for a coffee table or bench. Make top about $5\frac{1}{2}$" X 2 3/4".

a.   b.   c.

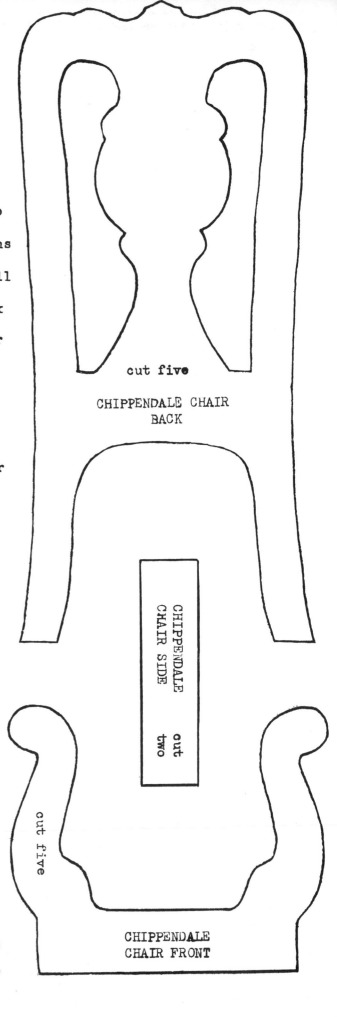

cut five

CHIPPENDALE CHAIR
BACK

CHIPPENDALE CHAIR SIDE   cut two

cut five

CHIPPENDALE
CHAIR FRONT

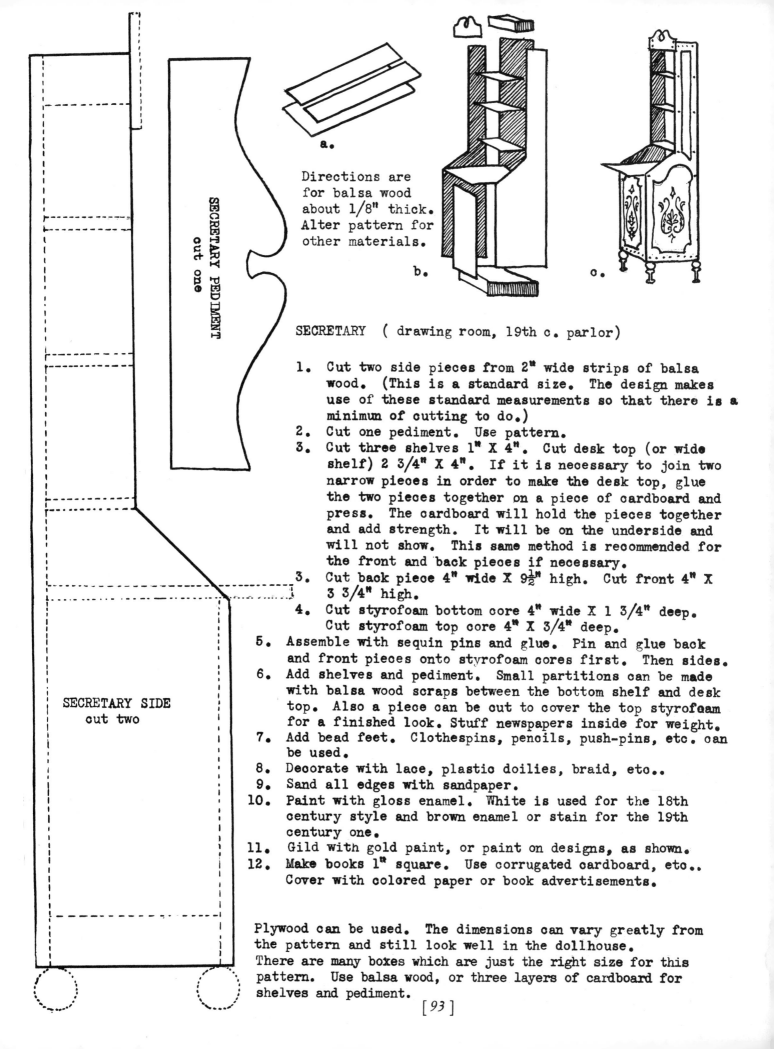

SECRETARY PEDIMENT
cut one

SECRETARY SIDE
cut two

Directions are for balsa wood about 1/8" thick. Alter pattern for other materials.

a.

b.

c.

SECRETARY (drawing room, 19th c. parlor)

1. Cut two side pieces from 2" wide strips of balsa wood. (This is a standard size. The design makes use of these standard measurements so that there is a minimum of cutting to do.)
2. Cut one pediment. Use pattern.
3. Cut three shelves 1" X 4". Cut desk top (or wide shelf) 2 3/4" X 4". If it is necessary to join two narrow pieces in order to make the desk top, glue the two pieces together on a piece of cardboard and press. The cardboard will hold the pieces together and add strength. It will be on the underside and will not show. This same method is recommended for the front and back pieces if necessary.
3. Cut back piece 4" wide X 9$\frac{1}{2}$" high. Cut front 4" X 3 3/4" high.
4. Cut styrofoam bottom core 4" wide X 1 3/4" deep. Cut styrofoam top core 4" X 3/4" deep.
5. Assemble with sequin pins and glue. Pin and glue back and front pieces onto styrofoam cores first. Then sides.
6. Add shelves and pediment. Small partitions can be made with balsa wood scraps between the bottom shelf and desk top. Also a piece can be cut to cover the top styrofoam for a finished look. Stuff newspapers inside for weight.
7. Add bead feet. Clothespins, pencils, push-pins, etc. can be used.
8. Decorate with lace, plastic doilies, braid, etc..
9. Sand all edges with sandpaper.
10. Paint with gloss enamel. White is used for the 18th century style and brown enamel or stain for the 19th century one.
11. Gild with gold paint, or paint on designs, as shown.
12. Make books 1" square. Use corrugated cardboard, etc.. Cover with colored paper or book advertisements.

Plywood can be used. The dimensions can vary greatly from the pattern and still look well in the dollhouse. There are many boxes which are just the right size for this pattern. Use balsa wood, or three layers of cardboard for shelves and pediment.

[93]

LOUIS XV END CHAIR (drawing room)

1. Cut five chair pieces from cardboard. (Use
   tablet-back or laundry cardboard)
2. Glue two of the pieces together.
3. Wrap them around a jar, can, etc.
4. Cover third piece with glue and wrap around the
   first two. Be sure to center the back and press
   around toward the front.
5. Each piece will fall short a little in the front.
   The legs will not match exactly but after the
   chair is dry, the unevenness can be
   trimmed away with a razor blade and
   sanded.
6. Glue and press on the fourth and
   then the fifth pieces in the same
   manner.
7. Tie securely with string till dry.
   Bend feet out slightly as
   indicated, while still damp.

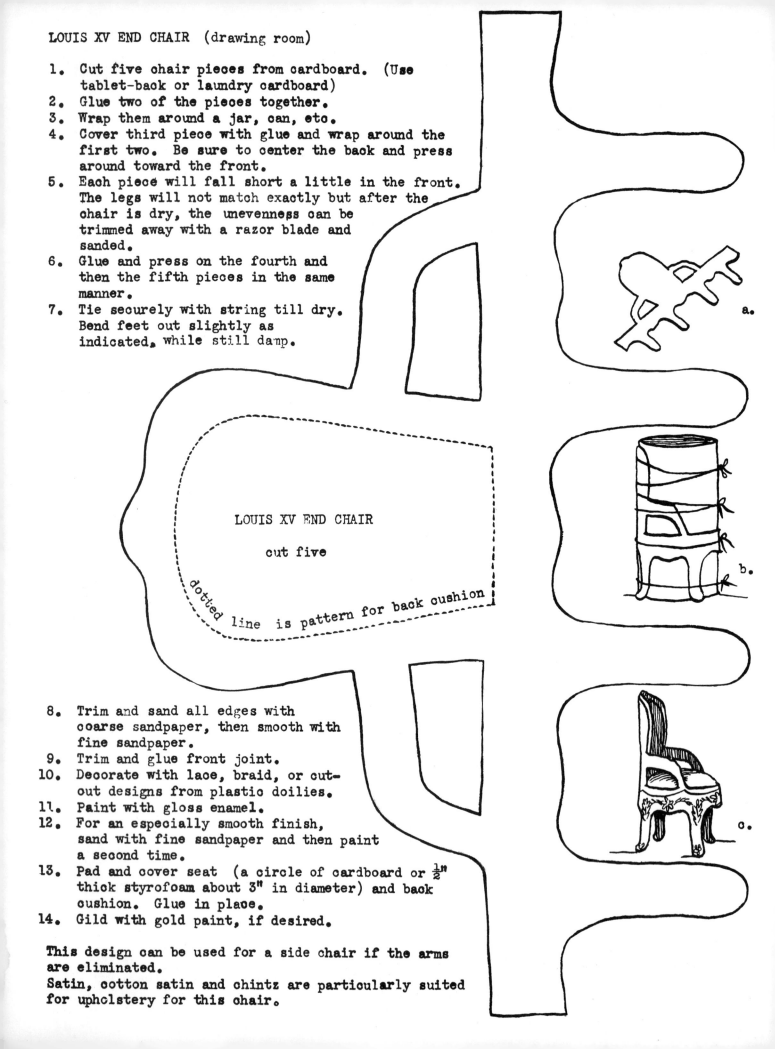

LOUIS XV END CHAIR

cut five

dotted line is pattern for back cushion

a.

b.

c.

8. Trim and sand all edges with
   coarse sandpaper, then smooth with
   fine sandpaper.
9. Trim and glue front joint.
10. Decorate with lace, braid, or cut-
    out designs from plastic doilies.
11. Paint with gloss enamel.
12. For an especially smooth finish,
    sand with fine sandpaper and then paint
    a second time.
13. Pad and cover seat (a circle of cardboard or $\frac{1}{2}$"
    thick styrofoam about 3" in diameter) and back
    cushion. Glue in place.
14. Gild with gold paint, if desired.

This design can be used for a side chair if the arms
are eliminated.
Satin, cotton satin and chintz are particularly suited
for upholstery for this chair.

19th CENTURY DESIGNS

19th century designs were elaborate and were inspired by many earlier types. Scrolls, tassels, flowers, swags, and plumes were popular. They were done in gold, black or sometimes even in full color.

Use them on tables, chairs, chests, cabinets, beds, wall panels, etc. Some can be used for stencils but they are actually intended for a pencil guide for painting on with a small brush.

Use metallic paint, enamel or water paints or inks. (Surface may need to be wiped with a damp cloth if paint rolls off.) Shellac or spray on clear fixative when dry to preserve decoration and to give an antique finish.

When making the furniture from plywood the designs can be used for guides for carving.

All of them can be used as additional needlework patterns for embroidering foot stools, wall hangings, linens, firescreens, curtains, upholstery, doll clothes, pillows, etc. Use all types of embroidery stitches.

These designs can be interchanged with the 18th century ones because most of them originated during the 18th century anyway. 19th century designers were known for copying early architecture and furniture.

[95]

BEDS, 19th CENTURY

Number 1 was made from a 12" X 6" piece of 1" thick styrofoam and two coat hangers. (A box or wood can be used.) Upholster the styrofoam completely, as though "wrapping a box." Use plenty of white glue. A heavy fabric will work best for this design. Unwind coathangers and cut or break at point where spiral begins. Start loop in the MIDDLE of hanger and utilize the corner bends which are already there. Leave ends straight and put through bed after small holes have been made with sharp tool, such as scissors point, large needle, etc.. Make loop for foot as indicated. Paint gold or black. Make mattress and linens to fit.

Number 2 was made with a box packed with folded newspapers, then glued together. The headboard was made with pencils, beads, and plastic doily. See needlework section for bedcover ideas.

Use five pencils with a bead (or push pin) glued and pinned into the eraser end. Slice off the eraser, even with the metal. Punch holes in bed frame for pencils and glue in place. It will be necessary to lay a book or board across the pencils to keep them in line while the glue dries. Stand the bed up on end for this. The decorative "brass" scrolls were made with part of a rectangular plastic doily, tied and glued in front of the pencils. Paint gold or black. A similiar headboard can be made with pants hanger tubes.

Number 3, shown in the 19th century nursery, was made of a sturdy box and two coathangers. The head and foot are similiar to no. 1 but with more elaborate loops. Be sure to start loops in the middle of the coathangers. After putting wire through the box, bend the end up against the side of the box to hold it in place. Paint gold or black.

Number 4 was also made from a sturdy box. Beads, cloth, and a brass drawer pull help to make it authentic 19th century. Old jewelery, or a brass cup hook can be used. Cut the top of the box in half, upholster each half, and glue to box which has been covered with the same cloth.

Number 5 was made from corrugated cardboard. See diagram for method of cutting the bed in one piece. Score with a razor blade or scissors so it will bend neatly. Use cloth strips for joints. Canopy is just a flat piece of the cardboard the same size as the finished bed frame. Posts can be made with heavy paper. Cover paper with glue and roll tightly. When dry it will be surprisingly hard.

Number 6 was made from a sturdy box (wood or styrofoam can be used) and a headboard made with the bureau pattern. This can be used with the bureau for a matched set like those popular during the Victorian era. See Victorian master bedroom.

Plywood can be used for all these designs, especially nos. 4 and 6.
Most boxes can be lengthened to fit the 12" dolls by adding wood or styrofoam before upholstering.

Use muslin for mattresses and batiste for linens. Be sure to monogram them for posterity!

VICTORIAN LADIES' CHAIR (master bedroom)

1. Use scouring powder can. (Salt box or cardboard can be used.) Place pattern and draw around it.
2. Cut with razor blade or kitchen knife.
3. Cut twenty leg pieces from laundry or tablet back cardboard. Glue and press in stacks of five layers each. When dry, sand and paint with brown gloss enamel. Cut three back decoration pieces, glue and press, sand and paint.
4. Add 3/4" around pattern for outside upholstery piece. Glue into place. Clip as indicated, glue clipped edges.
5. Cut cardboard for inside cushion. Pad and cover as indicated. Tuft with a needle and thread. (This chair can be upholstered without padding, if preferred. See FRENCH ARMCHAIR)
6. Glue inside cushion and chair together. Use clothes-pins, etc. to hold together till dry.
7. Cut seat 2 5/8" in diameter. Use 1" thick styrofoam. Pad and cover. Glue into place. (Put glue in chair, not on seat.)

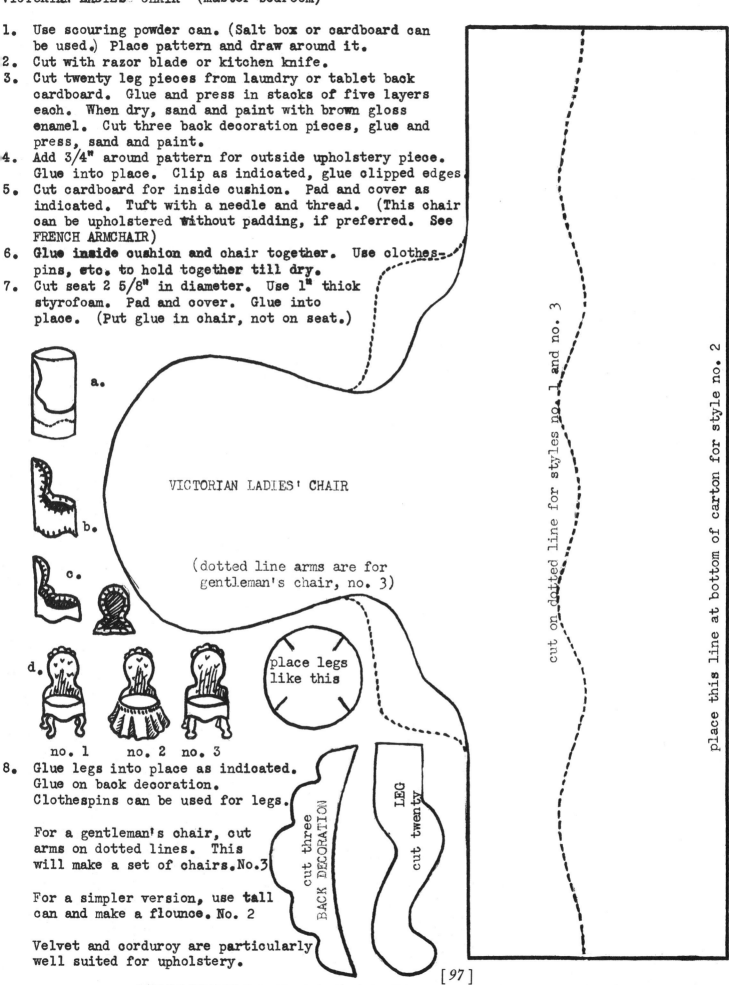

a.

b.

c.

VICTORIAN LADIES' CHAIR

(dotted line arms are for gentleman's chair, no. 3)

place legs like this

d.

no. 1   no. 2   no. 3

8. Glue legs into place as indicated. Glue on back decoration. Clothespins can be used for legs.

For a gentleman's chair, cut arms on dotted lines. This will make a set of chairs. No. 3

For a simpler version, use tall can and make a flounce. No. 2

Velvet and corduroy are particularly well suited for upholstery.

cut three
BACK DECORATION

LEG
cut twenty

cut on dotted line for styles no. 1 and no. 3

place this line at bottom of carton for style no. 2

[97]

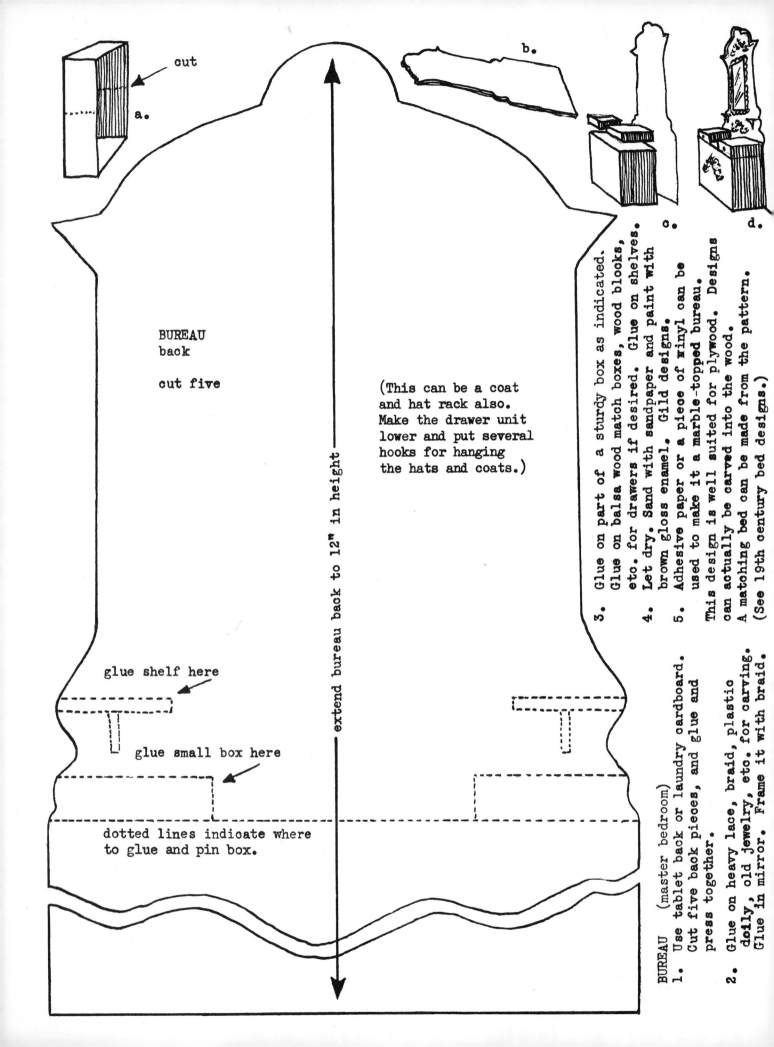

out

a.

b.

c.

d.

BUREAU
back

cut five

extend bureau back to 12" in height

(This can be a coat
and hat rack also.
Make the drawer unit
lower and put several
hooks for hanging
the hats and coats.)

glue shelf here

glue small box here

dotted lines indicate where
to glue and pin box.

BUREAU   (master bedroom)
1. Use tablet back or laundry cardboard.
    Cut five back pieces, and glue and
    press together.

2. Glue on heavy lace, braid, plastic
    dolly, old jewelry, etc. for carving.
    Glue in mirror. Frame it with braid.

3. Glue on part of a sturdy box as indicated.
    Glue on balsa wood match boxes, wood blocks,
    etc. for drawers if desired. Glue on shelves.

4. Let dry. Sand with sandpaper and paint with
    brown gloss enamel. Gild designs.

5. Adhesive paper or a piece of vinyl can be
    used to make it a marble-topped bureau.

This design is well suited for plywood. Designs
can actually be carved into the wood.
A matching bed can be made from the pattern.
(See 19th century bed designs.)

FEDERAL ROCKER   (nursery)

1. Cut ten chair side pieces. Use laundry or tablet back cardboard.
2. Cut seat and back pieces from $\frac{1}{2}$" thick styrofoam. Make seat $2\frac{1}{2}$" X 3". Make back $2\frac{1}{2}$" X 3 3/4".
3. Glue (with white glue) and press side pieces into two stacks of five each, till dry.
4. Sand edges with coarse sandpaper, then sand with fine sandpaper.
5. Paint with brown gloss enamel. When dry, sand with fine sandpaper and paint again for a smooth finish.
6. Pad and cover the back and seat pieces completely. Use white glue and cloth. The top edge of the back piece and the front edge of the seat piece should be rounded slightly. A dark fabric looks best on this chair. It can be embroidered to look like needlepoint. See needlework pages for patterns.
7. Assemble as indicated with glue and pins.

This chair can be made with plywood and then stained for a natural finish.

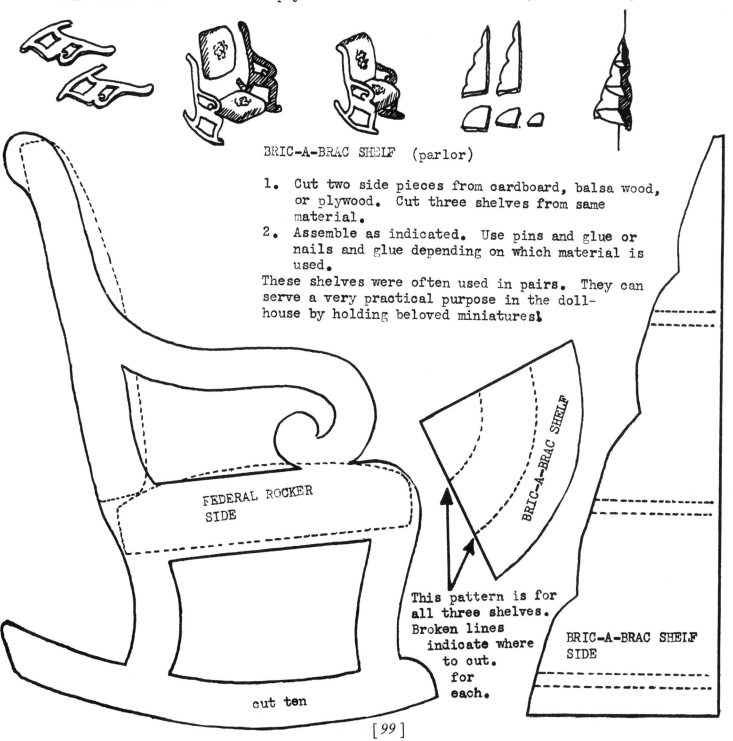

BRIC-A-BRAC SHELF   (parlor)

1. Cut two side pieces from cardboard, balsa wood, or plywood. Cut three shelves from same material.
2. Assemble as indicated. Use pins and glue or nails and glue depending on which material is used.

These shelves were often used in pairs. They can serve a very practical purpose in the doll-house by holding beloved miniatures!

FEDERAL ROCKER SIDE

BRIC-A-BRAC SHELF

This pattern is for all three shelves. Broken lines indicate where to cut for each.

BRIC-A-BRAC SHELF SIDE

cut ten

POT BELLIED STOVE (master bedroom)

1. Use plastic mustard bottle or any similiarly shaped container such as a toy bank, etc..
2. Cut stove base about 2½" X 2½" from balsa wood, wood, or several layers of cardboard. Cut hole for rim of bottle which should be put in up-side-down. Use beads for feet.
3. A stove top can be glued on if desired. Draw around the bottom of the bottle and add about ⅛" all around it. Use cardboard, wood, or balsa wood.
4. Use paper tube from pants hanger, or any ½" dowel for stove pipe. Cut about 8" long. Cut horizontal piece about 2" long. Cut pieces at an angle as indicated and join with glue. Add cardboard disc to finish off stove pipe. Pipe can enter stove at top or in the back. Cut hole and glue into place.
5. Paint entire stove black. Stove can be stuffed tightly with paper to give weight if desired.

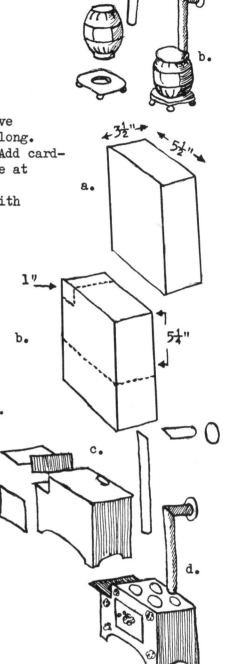

WOOD RANGE (kitchen, dining room)

1. Use box approximately 3½" deep by about 5½" wide such as those used for borax, starch, chocolate drink, etc..
2. Cut to about 5¼" high. Use the bottom part of the box in order to avoid the opening.
3. Measure about 1" square at the top left hand corner and cut away as indicated.
4. Fill in the cut away part with balsa wood or cardboard. Let shelf part extend past the edge slightly as indicated.
5. Cut out curved areas at the bottom of the stove as shown to give the look of legs. Fold a piece of paper and cut the curve to use as a pattern.
6. See no. 4 above for stove pipe.
7. Cut rectangle about 2½" X 3½" from wood, balsa wood or cardboard for door. Glue onto stove and press. Use bead for door handle. Glue on cardboard discs for top openings if desired.
8. Glue on lace, cut-outs from plastic doilies, or braid for decoration.
9. Paint entire stove black.

There is a charming toy iron stove available which is about the same proportion as this one.

DRY SINK (kitchen, dining room)

1. Use large size cocoa or chocolate drink box with metal top and lid.
2. Cut box about 5½" high so that the proportions are about the same as those of the stove. See above.
3. Remove the metal lid and fasten it from the under side of the hole with liquid solder.
4. Cut doors about 2" X 4" each from balsa wood or cardboard. Glue on and press. Use beads for knobs.
5. If shelf unit is used make it from balsa wood or cardboard and glue onto sink. It can be fastened to the wall if preferred, or eliminated altogether.
6. Paint with brown enamel. Leave metal part unpainted so it looks like the tin used in the old sinks.

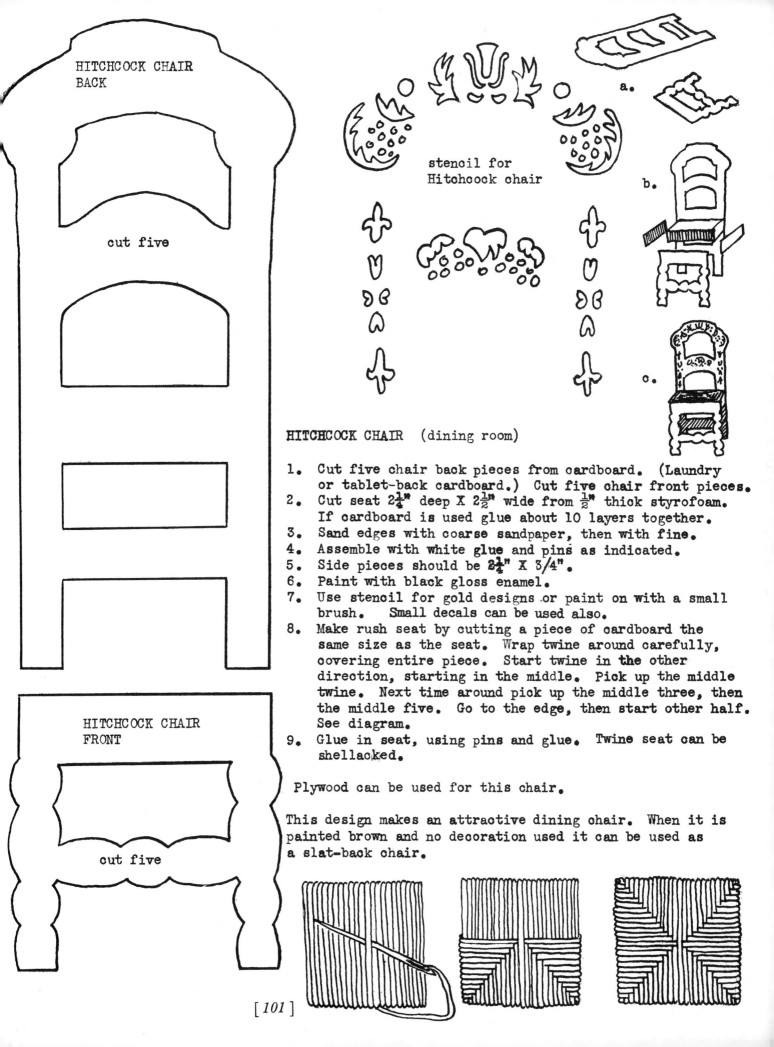

HITCHCOCK CHAIR
BACK

cut five

stencil for
Hitchcock chair

a.

b.

c.

HITCHCOCK CHAIR
FRONT

cut five

HITCHCOCK CHAIR   (dining room)

1. Cut five chair back pieces from cardboard. (Laundry or tablet-back cardboard.) Cut five chair front pieces.
2. Cut seat $2\frac{1}{4}$" deep X $2\frac{1}{2}$" wide from $\frac{1}{2}$" thick styrofoam. If cardboard is used glue about 10 layers together.
3. Sand edges with coarse sandpaper, then with fine.
4. Assemble with white glue and pins as indicated.
5. Side pieces should be $2\frac{1}{4}$" X 3/4".
6. Paint with black gloss enamel.
7. Use stencil for gold designs or paint on with a small brush.   Small decals can be used also.
8. Make rush seat by cutting a piece of cardboard the same size as the seat. Wrap twine around carefully, covering entire piece. Start twine in **the** other direction, starting in the middle. Pick up the middle twine. Next time around pick up the middle three, then the middle five. Go to the edge, then start other half. See diagram.
9. Glue in seat, using pins and glue. Twine seat can be shellacked.

Plywood can be used for this chair.

This design makes an attractive dining chair. When it is painted brown and no decoration used it can be used as a slat-back chair.

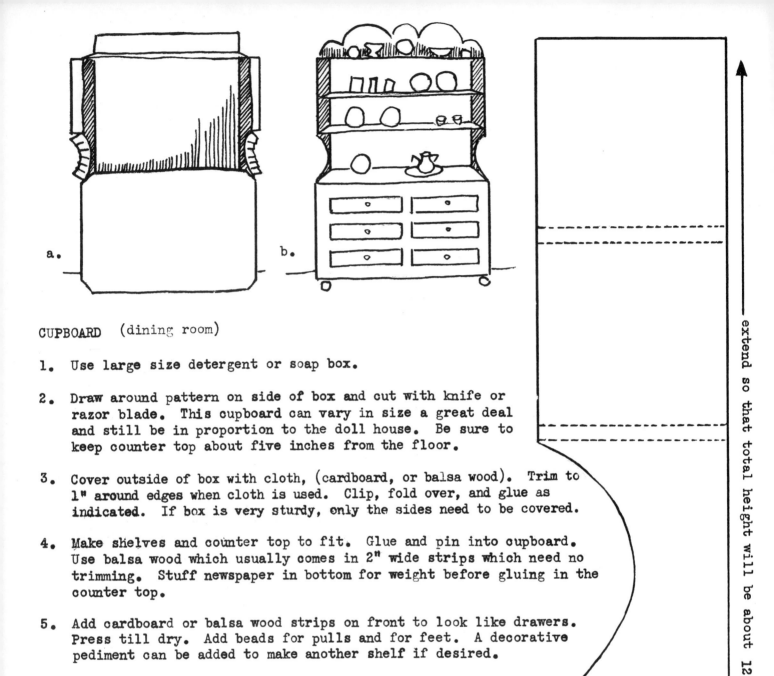

a.

b.

CUPBOARD (dining room)

1. Use large size detergent or soap box.

2. Draw around pattern on side of box and cut with knife or
   razor blade. This cupboard can vary in size a great deal
   and still be in proportion to the doll house. Be sure to
   keep counter top about five inches from the floor.

3. Cover outside of box with cloth, (cardboard, or balsa wood). Trim to
   1" around edges when cloth is used. Clip, fold over, and glue as
   indicated. If box is very sturdy, only the sides need to be covered.

4. Make shelves and counter top to fit. Glue and pin into cupboard.
   Use balsa wood which usually comes in 2" wide strips which need no
   trimming. Stuff newspaper in bottom for weight before gluing in the
   counter top.

5. Add cardboard or balsa wood strips on front to look like drawers.
   Press till dry. Add beads for pulls and for feet. A decorative
   pediment can be added to make another shelf if desired.

6. Paint with gloss enamel. If walls are
   painted, the same paint can be used on
   the cupboard for a built-in look.

This cupboard was designed for a very practical
purpose. A large cabinet with wide and deep
shelves is needed for the many miniatures which
will be collected. As in real homes, things
last longer when they have a place in which to
be stored! Good training, too, for future
homemakers!

This design is suitable for plywood. The
counter top can be hinged so that the bottom
part can be used for additional storage. The
counter top can be covered with vinyl or
adhesive paper for a "marble" top.

Doors can be made for the bottom part and shelves
added inside for storage when wood is used.

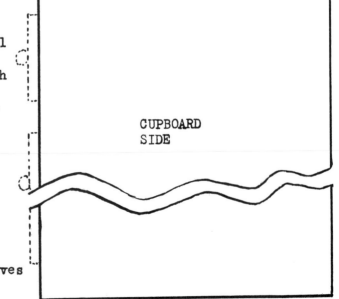

CUPBOARD
SIDE

extend so that total height will be about 12 inches

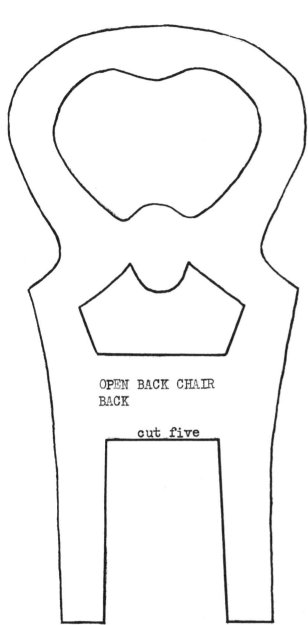

OPEN BACK CHAIR
BACK

cut five

This chair can be made with plywood
also. It can be carved and stained
for an authentic look.

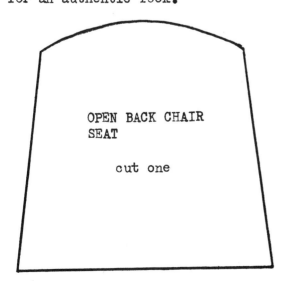

OPEN BACK CHAIR
SEAT

cut one

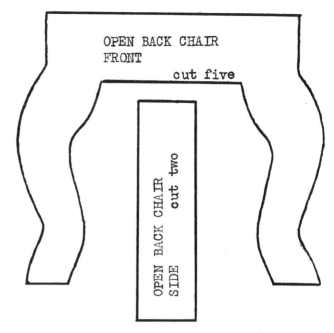

OPEN BACK CHAIR
FRONT

cut five

OPEN BACK CHAIR
SIDE
cut two

OPEN BACK CHAIR   (dining room)

1. Cut five back pieces and five front pieces.
    Use laundry or tablet-back cardboard.
2. Glue the pieces together. Immediately bend
    the back around a quart jar, can, etc. and
    tie securely with twine till dry. Bend back
    legs out just slightly. Press front pieces.
    (If plywood is used, the back will be used
    flat and the seat should be cut straight to fit.)
3. Cut seat from $\frac{1}{2}$" thick styrofoam. (Cardboard
    can be used. Glue about ten layers together.)
    Cut two side pieces from cardboard.
4. Small lace rosettes can be glued on for carving,
    if desired.
5. Sand all edges with coarse sandpaper, then with
    fine sandpaper.
6. Assemble with pins and glue, as indicated.
7. Paint with brown gloss enamel. (White enamel
    can be used for a French provincial style.)
    When dry, sand with fine sandpaper and then
    paint again for a smooth finish.
8. For the seat cushion, cut a piece of cardboard
    the same size as the seat. Pad and cover. Glue
    to seat. It will be necessary to tie or pin to
    chair till dry. The cloth can be embroidered
    to look like needlepoint. See needlework pages.

TABLES, 19th CENTURY (master bedroom, dining room, parlor)

1. Cut five of each pedestal section. (Use tablet-back or laundry cardboard). Glue and press till dry. Be sure to use correct line for the type of table you want: dining, coffee, or end table.
2. Sand with coarse sandpaper. Assemble pedestal.
3. Cut table top 5 3/8" in diameter for dining table, 5" in diameter for coffee table, or 3" square for end table. Cover top with cardboard, balsa wood, vinyl, etc. the same size. Press till dry. Table top should be $\frac{1}{2}$" thick styrofoam.
4. Glue on side or apron.
5. Glue top and pedestal together. Push pedestal up into styrofoam top for a secure fit.
6. Glue on lace, braid, plastic doily cut-outs, etc. for carving, if desired. Designs can be painted if preferred. (See "19th Century Designs".)
7. Paint with brown gloss enamel. A marble finish can be painted on while paint is wet. Dip a piece of thread into another color paint and wiggle and pull it across table top.
8. A small lace handkerchief makes an excellent table cloth!

The cardboard for the table top and apron can be cut from wood-patterned paper plates and shellacked after being glued and pressed onto the top.

Spools can be used for pedestals. Use a wooden button, balsa wood, etc. for base. Use large spools and a wooden coaster for large table. The coasters can be tops for end tables.

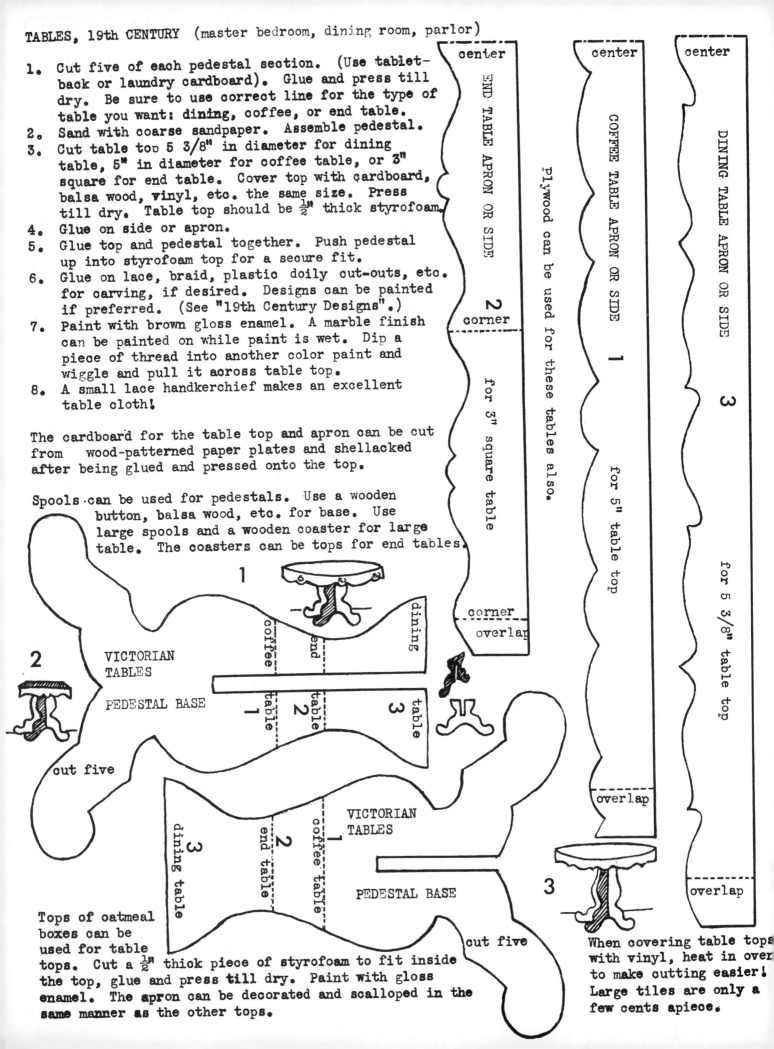

END TABLE APRON OR SIDE center 2 corner for 3" square table corner overlap

Plywood can be used for these tables also.

COFFEE TABLE APRON OR SIDE center 1 for 5" table top overlap

DINING TABLE APRON OR SIDE center 3 for 5 3/8" table top overlap

VICTORIAN TABLES PEDESTAL BASE coffee table 1 end table 2 dining table 3

cut five

VICTORIAN TABLES dining table 3 end table 2 coffee table 1 PEDESTAL BASE

cut five

Tops of oatmeal boxes can be used for table tops. Cut a $\frac{1}{2}$" thick piece of styrofoam to fit inside the top, glue and press till dry. Paint with gloss enamel. The apron can be decorated and scalloped in the same manner as the other tops.

When covering table tops with vinyl, heat in oven to make cutting easier! Large tiles are only a few cents apiece.

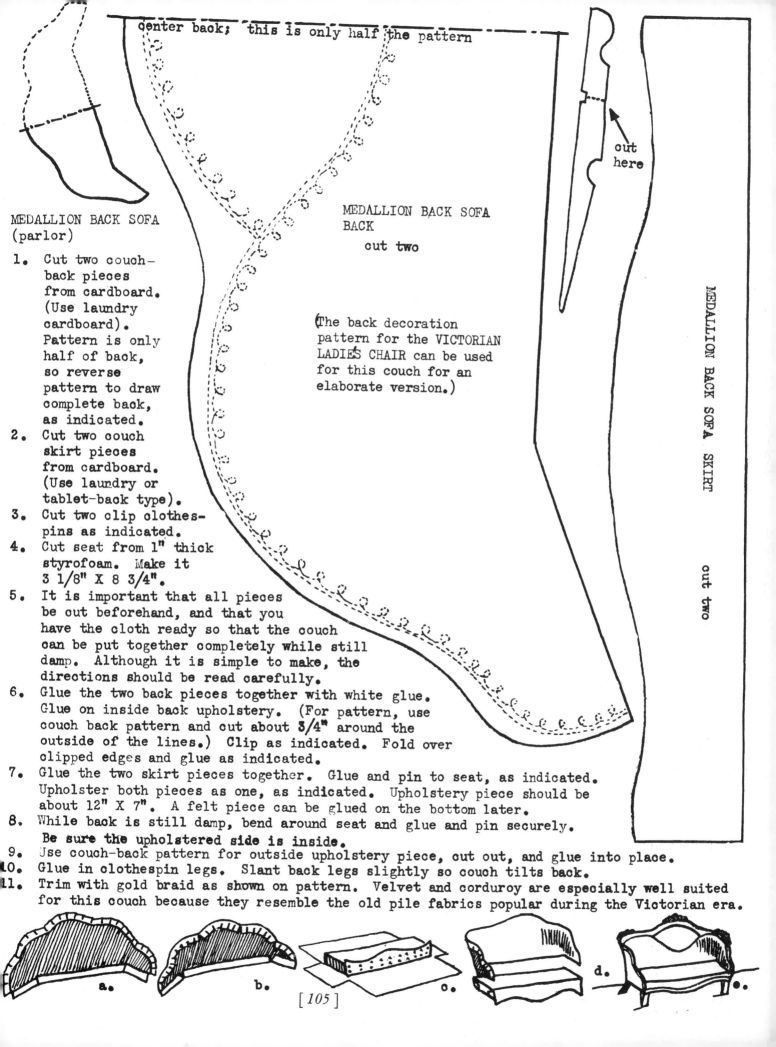

out here

MEDALLION BACK SOFA BACK
cut two

(The back decoration pattern for the VICTORIAN LADIES CHAIR can be used for this couch for an elaborate version.)

MEDALLION BACK SOFA SKIRT

cut two

MEDALLION BACK SOFA
(parlor)

1. Cut two couch-back pieces from cardboard. (Use laundry cardboard). Pattern is only half of back, so reverse pattern to draw complete back, as indicated.
2. Cut two couch skirt pieces from cardboard. (Use laundry or tablet-back type).
3. Cut two clip clothes-pins as indicated.
4. Cut seat from 1" thick styrofoam. Make it 3 1/8" X 8 3/4".
5. It is important that all pieces be cut beforehand, and that you have the cloth ready so that the couch can be put together completely while still damp. Although it is simple to make, the directions should be read carefully.
6. Glue the two back pieces together with white glue. Glue on inside back upholstery. (For pattern, use couch back pattern and cut about 3/4" around the outside of the lines.) Clip as indicated. Fold over clipped edges and glue as indicated.
7. Glue the two skirt pieces together. Glue and pin to seat, as indicated. Upholster both pieces as one, as indicated. Upholstery piece should be about 12" X 7". A felt piece can be glued on the bottom later.
8. While back is still damp, bend around seat and glue and pin securely. Be sure the upholstered side is inside.
9. Use couch-back pattern for outside upholstery piece, cut out, and glue into place.
10. Glue in clothespin legs. Slant back legs slightly so couch tilts back.
11. Trim with gold braid as shown on pattern. Velvet and corduroy are especially well suited for this couch because they resemble the old pile fabrics popular during the Victorian era.

a.   b.   c.   d.   e.

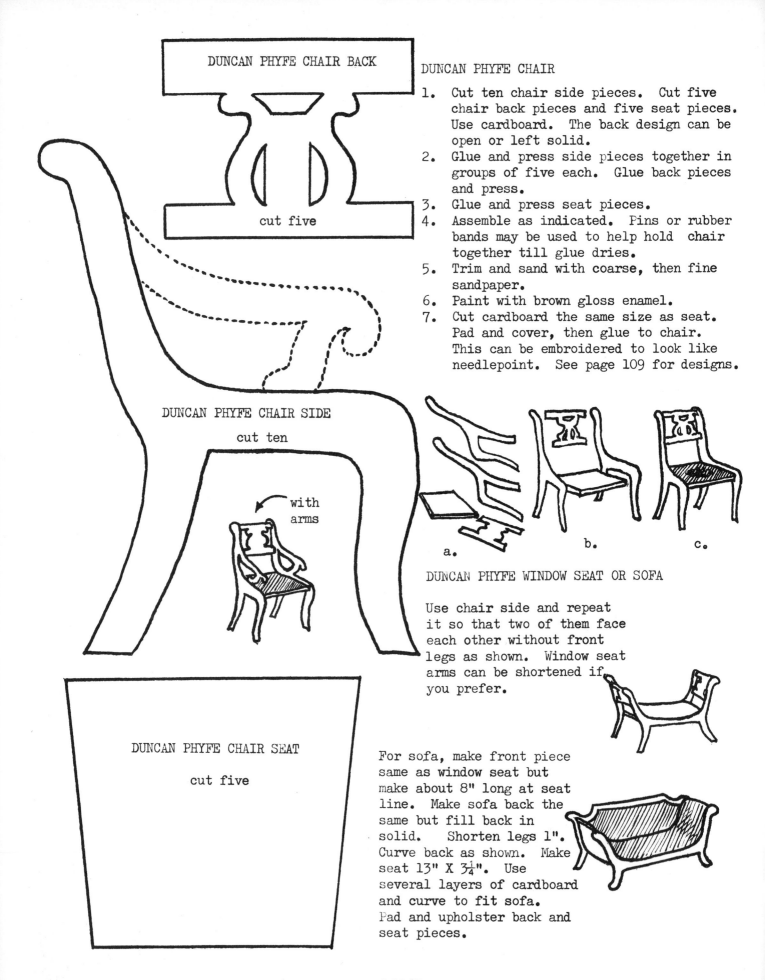

DUNCAN PHYFE CHAIR BACK

cut five

DUNCAN PHYFE CHAIR SIDE

cut ten

with
arms

DUNCAN PHYFE CHAIR SEAT

cut five

DUNCAN PHYFE CHAIR

1. Cut ten chair side pieces. Cut five chair back pieces and five seat pieces. Use cardboard. The back design can be open or left solid.
2. Glue and press side pieces together in groups of five each. Glue back pieces and press.
3. Glue and press seat pieces.
4. Assemble as indicated. Pins or rubber bands may be used to help hold chair together till glue dries.
5. Trim and sand with coarse, then fine sandpaper.
6. Paint with brown gloss enamel.
7. Cut cardboard the same size as seat. Pad and cover, then glue to chair. This can be embroidered to look like needlepoint. See page 109 for designs.

a.   b.   c.

DUNCAN PHYFE WINDOW SEAT OR SOFA

Use chair side and repeat it so that two of them face each other without front legs as shown. Window seat arms can be shortened if you prefer.

For sofa, make front piece same as window seat but make about 8" long at seat line. Make sofa back the same but fill back in solid. Shorten legs 1". Curve back as shown. Make seat 13" X 3¼". Use several layers of cardboard and curve to fit sofa. Pad and upholster back and seat pieces.

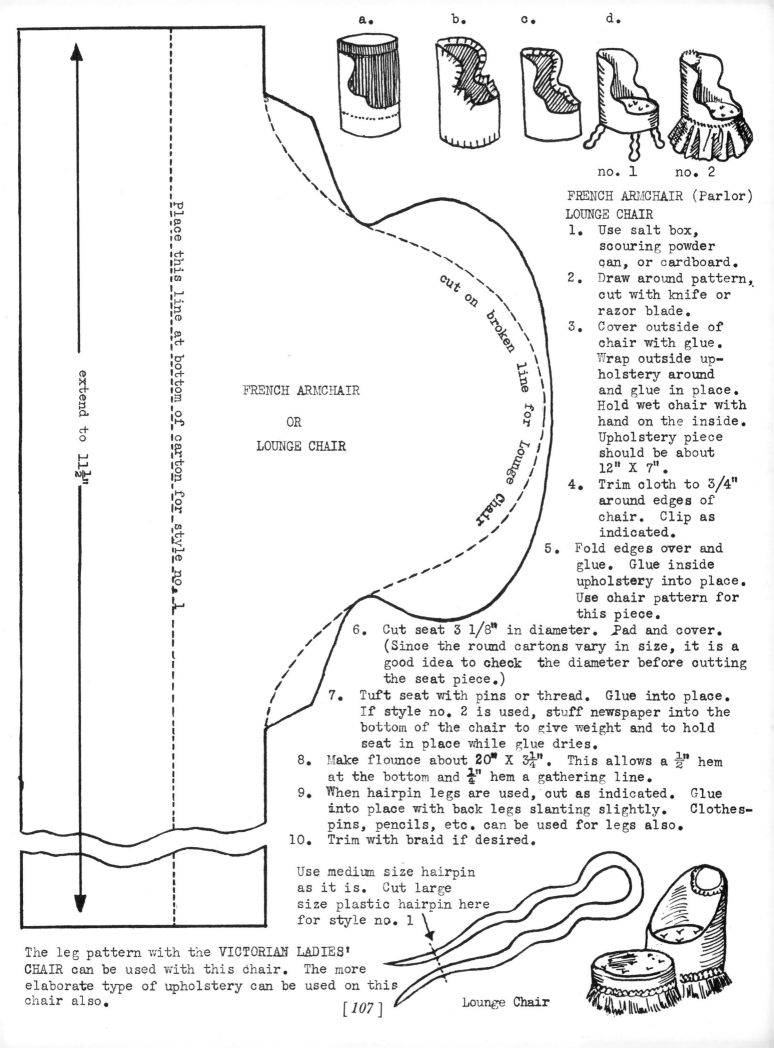

a. b. c. d.

no. 1   no. 2

FRENCH ARMCHAIR (Parlor)
LOUNGE CHAIR

1. Use salt box, scouring powder can, or cardboard.
2. Draw around pattern, cut with knife or razor blade.
3. Cover outside of chair with glue. Wrap outside upholstery around and glue in place. Hold wet chair with hand on the inside. Upholstery piece should be about 12" X 7".
4. Trim cloth to 3/4" around edges of chair. Clip as indicated.
5. Fold edges over and glue. Glue inside upholstery into place. Use chair pattern for this piece.
6. Cut seat 3 1/8" in diameter. Pad and cover. (Since the round cartons vary in size, it is a good idea to check the diameter before cutting the seat piece.)
7. Tuft seat with pins or thread. Glue into place. If style no. 2 is used, stuff newspaper into the bottom of the chair to give weight and to hold seat in place while glue dries.
8. Make flounce about 20" X 3¼". This allows a ½" hem at the bottom and ¼" hem a gathering line.
9. When hairpin legs are used, cut as indicated. Glue into place with back legs slanting slightly. Clothespins, pencils, etc. can be used for legs also.
10. Trim with braid if desired.

Use medium size hairpin as it is. Cut large size plastic hairpin here for style no. 1

FRENCH ARMCHAIR
OR
LOUNGE CHAIR

cut on broken line for Lounge Chair

Place this line at bottom of carton for style no. 1

extend to 11½"

The leg pattern with the VICTORIAN LADIES' CHAIR can be used with this chair. The more elaborate type of upholstery can be used on this chair also.

Lounge Chair

[107]

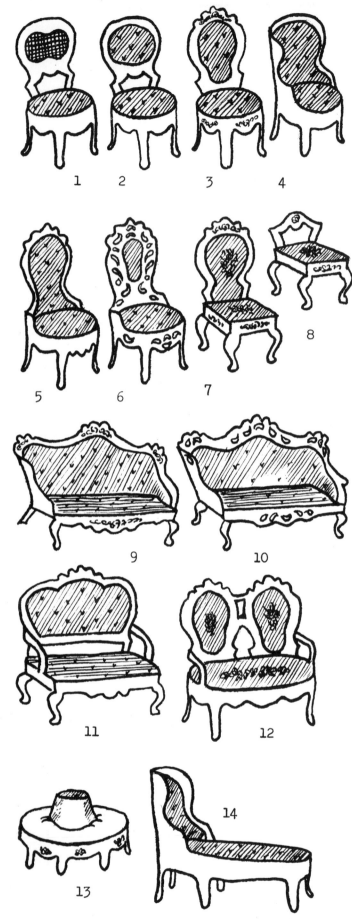

VARIATIONS, 19th CENTURY PATTERNS

1. CANE-BACK CHAIR Use lower part of chair on p. 94 with back of chair on p. 103. Use net or needlepoint canvas for caning.
2. VICTORIAN SIDE CHAIR Upholstery is used instead of caning as on no. 1.
3. ROSEWOOD CHAIR The same patterns as for no. 1 with back decoration on p. 97 added. Leave back solid, upholster and tuft.
4. VICTORIAN ARMCHAIR Use back and arms of p. 107 with chair on p. 94. Tuft with tiny beads and needle and thread.
5. BELTER CHAIR Use back, arms, and back decoration on p. 97 with chair on p. 94.
6. PIERCED BELTER CHAIR Make same as above and cut out designs as shown. Some of these chairs had upholstery on the back and some were all wood on the back.
7. VICTORIAN ROCOCO CHAIR Add back decoration on p. 97 to chair on p. 103 and leave back solid. Use front legs on back also and upholster as shown.
8. PARLOR OR VANITY CHAIR Make same as no. 7 and use only lower part of chair back.
9. BELTER SOFA Add back decoration on p. 97 to sofa back on p. 105. Use five layers of cardboard. Use front leg from p. 97. Glue on lace for carving. Use upholstery on inside and seat only. Curve front skirt as shown. Tuft upholstery with tiny beads.
10. PIERCED BELTER SOFA Make same as above, use leg on back also and cut out designs.
11. LOUIS XV LOVE SEAT Make same as chair no. 7 and stretch it to about 6" in length. Add arms. Back can be open.
12. ROSEWOOD SETTEE Make same as chair no. 3 and double it as shown. Add arms.
13. CIRCULAR SOFA Use two sets of leg section on p. 94 to make seat about 6½" in diameter and add center back rest as shown.
14. CHAISE LOUNGE Make same as no. 4 and stretch seat to about 8". Add legs in center.

1

2

3

4

5

6

fold on dotted line

NEEDLEPOINT DESIGNS

1, 2, & 3. These designs are used on so many throw pillows, stools, wall hangings, firescreens, linens, chair seats, etc., in 18th and 19th century houses that it is impossible to point them all out here. They are embroidered with a satin stitch. Dots are French knots. Those in the 19th century house are mostly done on velvet but any fabric is suitable. The designs look best when two shades of green are used for the leaves and a dark cloth is used for the background.
These designs can actually be worked in petit point.
Some stores carry kits for compact covers, eye glass covers, etc., which have designs small enough to use for miniatures in the doll houses.

CREWEL DESIGNS

4, & 5. (17th century house) These designs are for chair backs, footstools, linens, wall hangings, throw pillows, etc.. Any type embroidery stitch can be used for crewel work because it is an early type needlework. Most museums have examples that are primitive and charming.

CROSS-STITCH SAMPLER

6. (19th century master bedroom) The trees are done in outline stitch, French knots, and lazy daisy stitches. Be sure to put the date (where numbers are indicated on pattern) on your sampler for posterity. Cut a piece of cardboard the size of the dotted line area and fold edges of sampler over and glue on back. Add a string for hanging.
Use graph paper for designing your own original sampler. Be sure to sign your name for future reference.

Many notions counters carry designs which are already embroidered which need only to be stitched or glued onto the miniatures.

Many fabrics have designs which can be cut out and used instead of doing your own. Some fabric designs actually imitate needlepoint and crewel work.

A cross-stitch sampler can be worked on small checked gingham. Use printed patterns which are small enough, or design your own. This method is recommended for beginners because it is easy to keep the design straight.

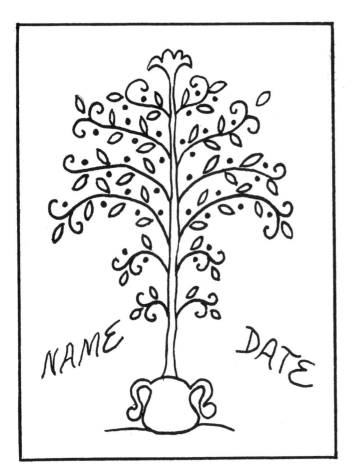

Number 1 WALL HANGING
Use muslin or broadcloth. Allow for a hem
on all sides. Use outline, lazy daisy,
and French knot stitches. Add the owner's
name and the date just for fun. Put
applicator sticks, or matchstems through
top and bottom hems. Tie cord for hanging.

Number 2 EMBROIDERED RUG
Use felt for rug. Use satin stitch and
French knots for border. Use satin stitch
and outline for eagle and banner. Use
outline and lazy daisy stitches for branches.
Put on the name of the owner and the date,
for future generations.

The embroidered rug was one of the first
rugs which had pictures. This type was
earlier than the hooked rug.

This rug can actually be done in petit point.

Both the "tree of life" wall hanging and
the rug are suitable for all three styles
of doll furniture. The eagle and the tree
have remained popular through the centuries.

NEEDLEPOINT RUG

Number 1 (See 18th century nursery) This rug can be made quickly and easily. It is all done in outline and lazy daisy stitches on felt. It is suitable for an oval or a rectangle. Velvet, wool, terry cloth, etc. can be used.

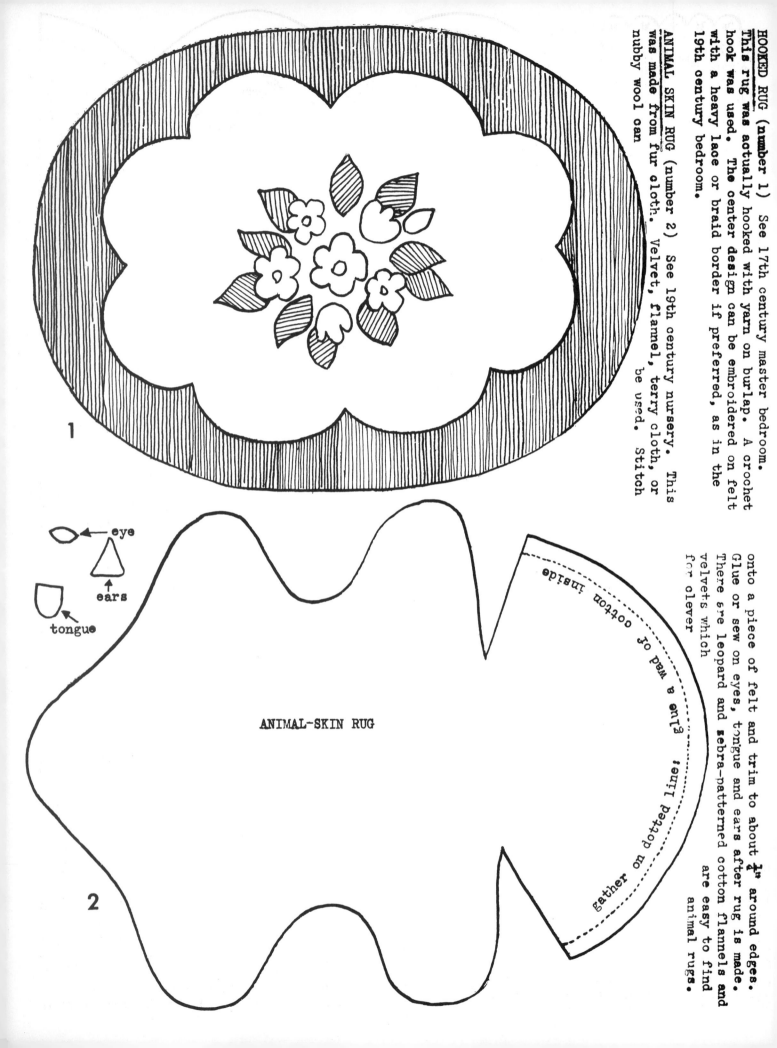

HOOKED RUG (number 1) See 17th century master bedroom. This rug was actually hooked with yarn on burlap. A crochet hook was used. The center design can be embroidered on felt with a heavy lace or braid border if preferred, as in the 19th century bedroom.

ANIMAL SKIN RUG (number 2) See 19th century nursery. This was made from fur cloth. Velvet, flannel, terry cloth, or nubby wool can be used. Stitch onto a piece of felt and trim to about ¼" around edges. Glue or sew on eyes, tongue and ears after rug is made. There are leopard and zebra-patterned cotton flannels and velvets which are easy to find for clever animal rugs.

1

eye

ears

tongue

ANIMAL-SKIN RUG

gather on dotted line, glue a pad of cotton inside

2

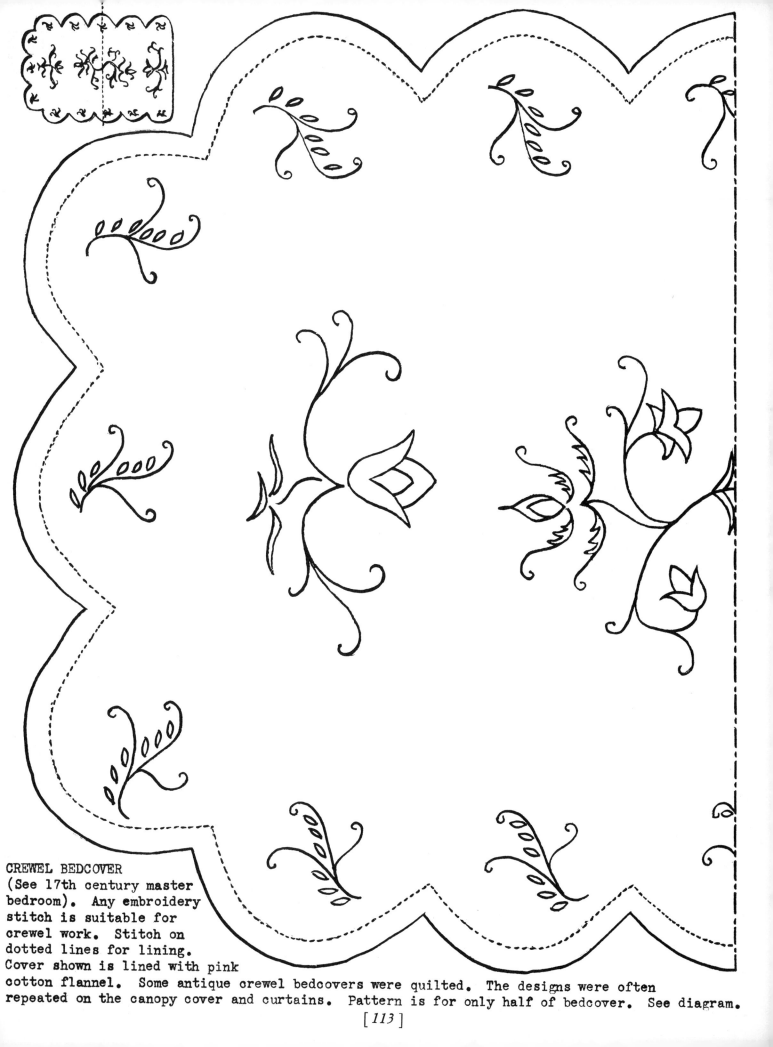

CREWEL BEDCOVER
(See 17th century master
bedroom). Any embroidery
stitch is suitable for
crewel work. Stitch on
dotted lines for lining.
Cover shown is lined with pink
cotton flannel. Some antique crewel bedcovers were quilted. The designs were often
repeated on the canopy cover and curtains. Pattern is for only half of bedcover. See diagram.

[113]

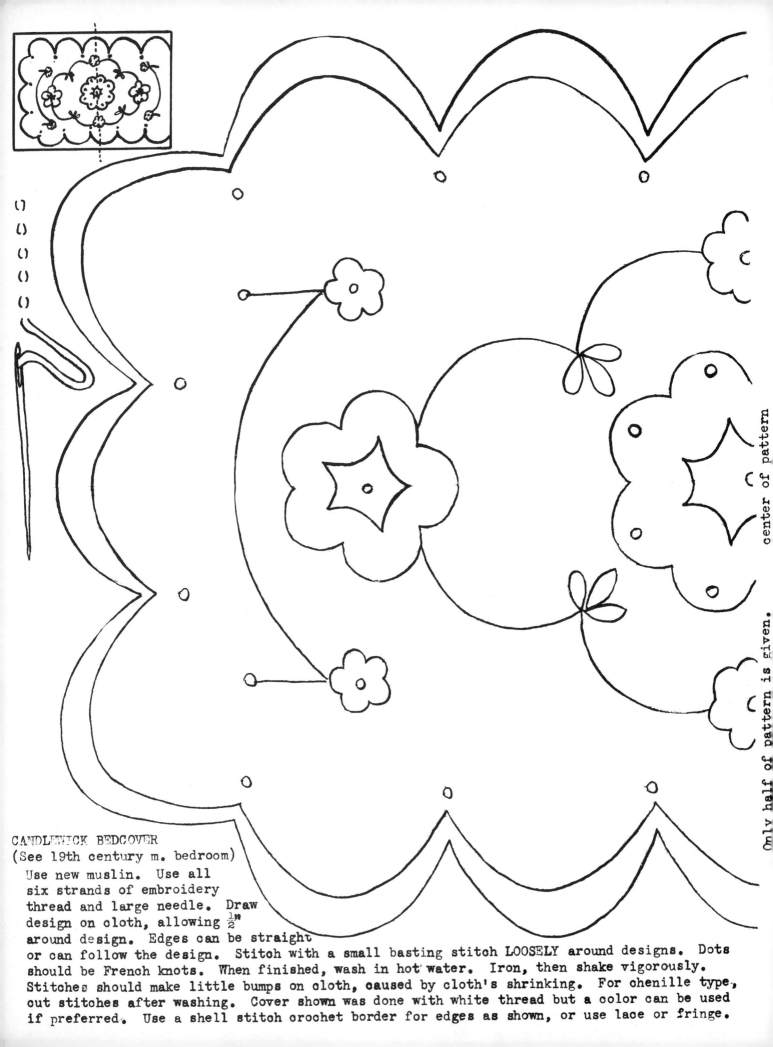

CANDLEWICK BEDCOVER
(See 19th century m. bedroom)
Use new muslin. Use all
six strands of embroidery
thread and large needle. Draw
design on cloth, allowing $\frac{1}{2}$"
around design. Edges can be straight
or can follow the design. Stitch with a small basting stitch LOOSELY around designs. Dots
should be French knots. When finished, wash in hot water. Iron, then shake vigorously.
Stitches should make little bumps on cloth, caused by cloth's shrinking. For chenille type,
cut stitches after washing. Cover shown was done with white thread but a color can be used
if preferred. Use a shell stitch crochet border for edges as shown, or use lace or fringe.

center of pattern

Only half of pattern is given.

1. Cooking pot from spray can or catsup top and hairpin. 2. Canisters from vitamin sample or pill bottles. 3. Plate holder from hairpin. 4. Chamber vases from spray can or catsup bottle cap and curtain rings with buttons for lids. Decorate with decals or paint. 5. Hip bath from plastic cup. 6. Trays from cocoa can lids. 7. Books and magazines from advertisements. 8. Churn from plastic medicine bottle and applicator stick. 9. Vase from lipstick case. 10. Clothes basket from bottom of large oval plastic lotion bottle. 11. "Band boxes" or hat boxes from zipper cases. 12. Foot warmer from match box and beads. 13. Cutting board from balsa wood. 14. Cake cover from deep lid and bead. 15. Wall candle box from lipstick case and two cup hooks. 16. Tiny sponges or throw pillows from sponges. 17. Bath and hair brushes from mascara brushes. 18. Colanders from plastic shaker tops and beads. 19. Paper towel and tissue holders from hairpins. 2o. Wall sconce from balsa wood. 21. Folding screen from 3 sections of cardboard glued onto a cloth. 22. Pictures from playing cards. 23. Bible box from aspirin box. 24. Towel ring from drawer pull. 25. Milking stool from balsa wood and match stems. 26. Trunk from recipe file box. 27. Liquid dishwashing soap cap will make: a. cake pan or gelatin mold, b. candle holder, c. ink well, d. candle holder, e. compote, f. cake stand, g. compote, h. candle holder, i. cake cover, j. candle holder. 28. Compact or purse mirrors with braid trim. 29. Spoon rack from balsa wood.

30. Cradle from basket and balsa wood. 31. Picture frames from cocoa box tops. 32. Clocks from toy watches and balsa wood. 33. Picture frames from curtain rings. Add trim or put on a ribbon. 34. Waste baskets and umbrella stands from detergent bottle caps, curlers, pill bottles. 35. Wall planters and salt box from match boxes. 36. Firescreen from cardboard, applicator stick and pill bottle cap. 37. Bed warmer from applicator stick and pill bottle caps. 38. Hearth broom from applicator stick and broom straws. 39. Lamps from: bottle with nut cup shade, door stop with cork shade, tooth paste tube shoulder with pencil and cork or styrofoam ball, Corks, ping-pong balls, or rubber balls on tooth paste tube shoulder base. Cork or ball on curtain hook for wall lamp. 40. Tooth paste caps for vases, flower pots and drinking beakers. 41. Wall shelf box from small box and balsa wood. 42. Bassinet from box, balsa wood and batiste. 43. Candle holder from soda pop bottle cap with hairpin handle attached with liquid solder. 44. Candle holder from chrome drawer pull. 45. Topiary tree from bottle cap, applicator stick and styrofoam ball with glitter. 46. Vase from doll bottle. 47. Cup hooks for hanging pots and pans, clothes, etc. 48. Powder horn from sweetener bottle cap. 49. Miniature food packages from food ads and bits of balsa wood and styrofoam. 50. Doughnuts from oat cereal. 51. Animal cookies from cereal in pill bottle cooky jars. 52. Plate and cup rack from hairpin or wire. 53. Picture frame from earring. 54. Picture frame from cardboard or balsa wood trimmed with gold braid. 55. Broom from typewriter brush eraser. 56. Cooky cutters from tiny aspic cutters. 57. Gelatin mold from miniature aspic-jelly mold. 58. Throw pillows from powder puffs. 59. Plate from shallow lid. 60. Beaker from sample lipstick case or metal cap.

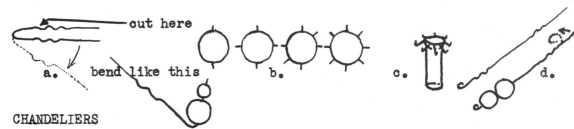

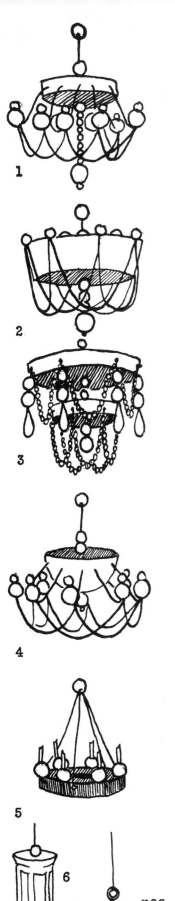

CHANDELIERS

a. Cut and bend small hairpins as indicated. They can be cut separately but should all be bent at once so they will match.

b. When gluing hairpins into place, start with two, opposite each other. Then place next two between them. Each time divide the remaining space in half. This way, when all are in place, they will be even. Six hairpins are more difficult to arrange than eight.

c. If the styrofoam is placed on a glass or bottle during assembly, the hairpins can be arranged evenly and they will remain undisturbed while drying.
After hairpins have been glued into place, paint styrofoam with white glue. Cover wet styrofoam with glitter.
When glitter is dry, chains and beads can be added. Put chains or strings of beads on first. Then slip on larger beads to look like lights. When hanging chains, hook onto every other hairpin. Then go around again hooking onto those skipped the first time. Glue chains and beads into place one at a time by sliding off and putting a drop of glue on the hairpin. Repeat around the rest.

d. For center wire, straighten out a hairpin or use twine, wire, or jewelry chain. Thread on or attach several beads, then thread up through the center of the styrofoam. Put on another bead or two and glue into place. Make a loop or put on a chain link at the top for hooking onto the ceiling hook.

no. 1. (See 19th century master bedroom). Use a disc of $\frac{1}{2}$" thick styrofoam, eight hairpins, and beads. See above method.

no. 2. (See 17th century living room). This style, made on a larger scale with beads, is used in the 18th and 19th century living rooms. Pins are used instead of hairpins.

no. 3. (See 18th century master bedroom). This style is a more difficult type, not recommended for beginners. Two styrofoam discs, one smaller than the other should be used. The beads must be strung especially for the chandelier because beads stiffen when draped. Tie and glue the strings onto pins which have been glued into the sides of the discs.

no. 4. (See 18th and 19th century nurseries. See 18th and 19th century dining rooms for this type with crystal beads.) This is the same as no. 1 except that half a styrofoam ball is used instead of a disc.

no. 5. (See 17th century kitchen) Cut a doughnut-shaped piece of styrofoam about 3" in diameter. Pin and glue on four chains for hanging. Join with loop or chain link at top. Use six or eight large beads with toothpicks stuck through them for candles. Glue in. Spray black.
Plastic birthday candle holders can be used instead of beads so real candles can be used!

nos. 6 & 7. (See 17th century bedrooms) A spool can be used for a Colonial lantern. Use beads and wire, twine, or jewelry chains. Paint with brush. Some dime stores carry a window shade pull which is a miniature lantern.

Use brass cup hooks in ceiling for attaching chandeliers. The hook allows the owner to change the chandeliers from one room to another.

[*117*]

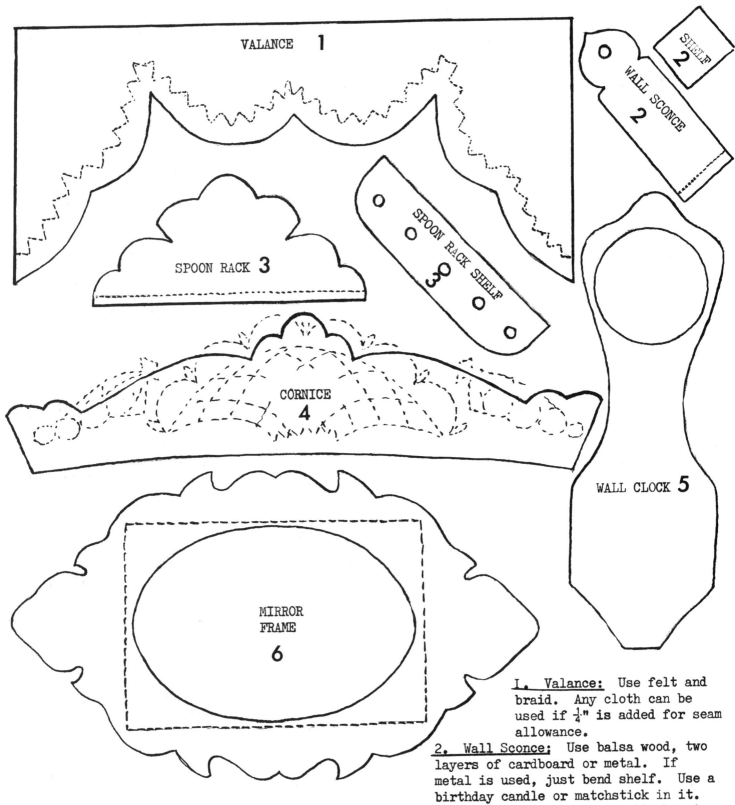

VALANCE 1

SHELF 2

WALL SCONCE 2

SPOON RACK 3

SPOON RACK SHELF 3

CORNICE 4

WALL CLOCK 5

MIRROR FRAME 6

1. **Valance:** Use felt and braid. Any cloth can be used if $\frac{1}{4}$" is added for seam allowance.

2. **Wall Sconce:** Use balsa wood, two layers of cardboard or metal. If metal is used, just bend shelf. Use a birthday candle or matchstick in it.

3. **Spoon Rack:** Use balsa wood, three layers of cardboard or metal. Paint gold, black, etc.

4. **Cornice:** Use balsa wood, plywood or three layers of cardboard. Decorate with cut-outs from plastic doilies, lace or braid for an authentic " pierced brass cornice." Paint gold.

5. **Wall Clock:** Use plywood, balsa wood, or cardboard (about six layers). Make hole for boy's toy watch. Check diameter of watch before cutting hole. Decorate with old jewelry. Styrofoam can be used if it is covered with cardboard and then painted.

6. **Mirror Frame:** Use cardboard or balsa wood. Cut two layers with rectangle cut-out. Cut one with oval cut-out. Glue all three together with oval on top. Press till dry. Purse mirror will fit into rectangle from back side and will appear to be an oval mirror from the front. Decorate with doilies, lace, braid, or old jewelry. Paint gold.

Index to Dolls

Appendix

TOOLS, EQUIPMENT, AND MATERIALS

Although most of the furniture designs can easily be adapted to wood and power tools, they are intended for simple materials and household tools such as these listed below.

paring knife—for cutting cartons, boxes and styrofoam.

scissors—for cutting cardboard, cloth, etc.

razor blade—(or art cutting knife from art or hobby stores) for cutting balsa wood, styrofoam, cardboard, etc. Be sure to use single-edge type.

[*119*]

pliers with wire cutting edge—for cutting pencils, clothespins, hairpins and coathangers. (Coathangers can be broken by bending back and forth, and the clothespins can be broken. Small hairpins can be used without cutting. That is why the pliers are not absolutely esential, but are a great help if you have them.)

sandpaper—for laminated cardboard and balsa wood. Use several pieces from coarse to fine.

paint and/or shellac—for all types of furniture. Small cans may be purchased in dime stores and hardware and paint stores for a few cents. You will probably need a small can of solvent also. The store clerk can give you the correct type for the paint you buy.

white glue—for gluing all types of materials. Can be found in dime stores, grocery stores, hobby stores, etc.

fabric—any type. Patterns give approximate amounts.

styrofoam—for furniture, seats of cardboard furniture, tables, etc. This is not absolutely essential and substitutes such as cardboard, wood, balsa wood, etc., are given on patterns. It can be found in many dime stores and most hobby and craft stores.

balsa wood—for furniture and some miniatures and accessories. Cardboard or wood can be substituted if preferred as suggested on the patterns. It can be purchased in most craft and hobby shops and some dime stores.

cardboard—for furniture, accessories, architectural panelling, etc. The coarse absorbent type used for tablet backs, in laundry packages, as stiffening in new clothes, large boxes such as those for coats and dresses, in fact any cardboard which is thin enough to be cut with scissors. Large sheets of cardboard can be bought in art stores for only a few cents a sheet if you prefer not to use discards.

small brush—for gluing and painting. Most dime stores have them for a few cents apiece. They also come in inexpensive water color sets.

clothespins—for furniture legs. The spring clip type can be found in most dime stores, grocery stores, and in most all mail order catalogues. Substitutes are usually given on patterns if you do not have any.

sequin pins—for constructing furniture. These are better than regular straight pins because they are only about ½″ long and do not bend when pushed into balsa wood, cardboard, etc. They can be found in dime stores, art and hobby stores, and notions counters in department stores.

match stems—for use in constructing styrofoam furniture and for various uses on other types of furniture. Be sure to strike matches over a sink and break off heads before using at your work place. Other small dowels such as applicator sticks (from the drugstore) can be used.

various cartons and boxes—for furniture. See individual patterns for suggestions. Substitutes are given on the patterns if other materials are preferred.

corrugated cardboard—for some furniture and for box room. Use large boxes which can be found at your grocery and other stores.

SCALE	SIZE OF SQUARES	
1" to 1'	$\frac{1}{4}$"	for dollhouses
1$\frac{1}{2}$" to 1'	$\frac{3}{8}$"	for dollhouses
* 2" to 1'	$\frac{1}{2}$"	for dollhouses
4" to 1'	1"	for large dolls, 15" to 26" tall
8" to 1'	2"	for real children for playhouses
12" to 1'	3"	life size, for reducing to dollhouse
		or playhouse size.

* This is the scale of the patterns in THE DOLLHOUSE BOOK.

To change the scale of a pattern in the book just draw a grid with $\frac{1}{2}$" squares over it as shown below. Next, check the chart to find what size grid you need for the desired scale, and draw it on another paper. Copy the pattern on the new grid so that it has the same relationship to the squares. The pattern shown reduced is the Chippendale Table on page 84.

Many dollhouses are either a 1" to 1' scale or the slightly larger 1$\frac{1}{2}$" to 1' scale.

For making doll furniture for larger dolls, about 15" to 26" tall, use the 4" to 1' scale on the chart. Use 1" squares for this.

The patterns can be enlarged still more so that they are large enough for playhouse furniture for real live children! This is the 8" to 1' scale on the chart. Use wood for making furniture this large.

The life-size scale is 12" to 1' and although the patterns can be enlarged this much, the scale is actually given so that it can be used in reverse. A life-size furniture pattern can be reduced by drawing a grid over the pattern with 3" squares and then drawing it again on smaller squares according to the chart.

The chart is planned also, so that you can enlarge a small-scale dollhouse item to the same scale as those in the book. The chart can be used for changing any pattern you may already have to either a larger or smaller size.

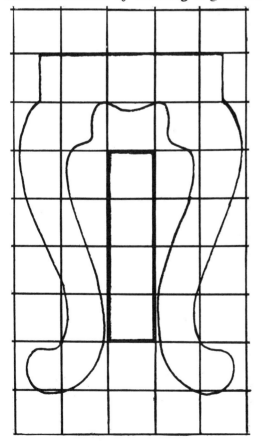 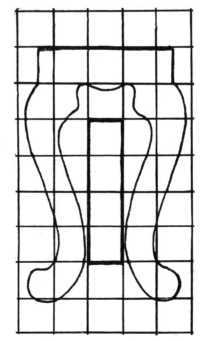 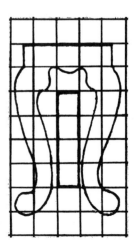

Chippendale Table (page 84) above reduced to 1$\frac{1}{2}$" to 1' scale, then to 1" to 1' scale.

Index

Numbers in *italic* type refer to pattern pages

[*123*]

[*125*]

Furniture and accessories

McIntyre's, 131 South San Gabriel Blvd., San Gabriel, California 91776.

Old dolls and dollhouse furniture and accessories. Send stamp for list. Interested in any you have for sale: prices and full description with first letter. Mildred Dix, 88 Allen Street, Walpole, Massachusetts 02081.

Peniston Doll Hospital, 210 Alexander Avenue, Los Gatos, California 95030. 25¢ for furniture list; 25¢ for accessory list; 25¢ for store units, merchandise and accessories; 10¢ each for lighting, bar and bar accessories, doll and dollhouse dolls lists.

Chestnut Hill Studio, Box 38, Churchville, New York 14428. Furniture and accessories. Wide range and high quality. New catalog (50¢) due in 1965.

Mrs. Mell Prescott, Milridge Road, Somers, Connecticut 06071. Custom-made furniture, and accessories.

Dorothy S. Weil, Sandwich, Massachusetts 02563. Small selection of accessories and furniture.

Margaret Whitton, 419 Danbury Road, Wilton, Connecticut 06897. Antique furniture, dolls, and books.

Dollhouse Delights, 302 Southeast Payton, Des Moines, Iowa 50315. Antique and modern furniture and accessories. Also copies of old magazines with doll and dollhouse articles.

Accessories

The Miniature Mart, 883-39th Avenue, San Francisco, California. Exact copies of those in Maynard Manor collection.

Furniture

Mrs. Opal Green, Route #1, Ashland, Missouri. Write for information and prices, send stamp.

Mrs. J. S. Waller, 14448 N. W. 16th Drive, Miami, Florida. Custom-made Victorian furniture. Real marble tops. She will cut one to fit your pattern.

Dollhouse Dolls

Dollhouse dolls, Community and family sets, also imported dolls and accessories. Dollhouses, furniture, books, articles. List 25¢ Sandcraft Industries, 3314 Paulding Avenue, Bronx, New York 10469.

Dollhouse Dolls by Eleanor-Jean Carter, Write Carter Craft Doll House, 5505 42nd Avenue, Hyattsville, Maryland 20781.

Doll House Dolls. Lovely Porcelain Reproductions. House of Dolls, 21343 Mission Blvd., Hayward, California 94541.

Light Fixtures, Accessories

Peniston's, 210 Alexander Avenue, Los Gatos, California 95030.

Materials

Plywood for miniatures and dollhouses. ⅛ inch Japanese ash-3 ply. Four (4) pieces 6 inches wide, 36 inches long. Sent postpaid for $2.50. Grab-bag of ¼ inch plywood pieces. Prefinished one side. Walnut, birch, cherry, mahogany. Various size pieces. Total of 5 square feet for $2.50, postpaid. Jack Fixit. 4235 East 10th Lane, Hialeah, Florida 33013.

Wallpaper for dollhouses. Imported. Helen Irene's, P. O. Box 19, Venice, California 90293.

Wee'ndle, P. O. Box 912, Opa Locka, Florida. Well-made and reasonably priced brass pulls, brass hinges with nails, and Victorian tear drop pulls.